MEET THE
SKEPTIC

A Field Guide to Faith Conversations

written and designed by **BILL FOSTER**

First printing: February 2012
Second printing: July 2014

Master Books®, P.O. Box 726, Green Forest, AR 72638
Master Books® is a division of the New Leaf Publishing Group, Inc.

ISBN: 978-0-89051-651-5
Library of Congress Control Number: 2009924369

Please consider requesting that a copy of this volume be purchased by your local library system.

For information regarding author interviews, please contact the publicity department at (870) 438-5288

Cover images provided by iStock.com

Cover design & book layout:
Bill Foster / HigherWerks: Brand image+Design / www.higherwerks.com

Master Books®
A Division of New Leaf Publishing Group
www.masterbooks.net

THANKS

One of the most profound ways God has shown His love for me is to surround me with godly parents, family, and a large group of close friends my entire life. Not everyone can say that and it is a blessing. Many thanks to them for supporting me in general and in particular during the writing of this book (a few friends in alphabetical order: Curt Dean, Dr. Joe Giaritelli, The Homies, Barrett Riddleberger, and Chris Swan).

Thanks to the following people for their contributions: Alex McFarland (Faith In Focus, Stand Strong); Steve Wright (InQuest Ministries); Martin Hester (Avisson Press); Kevin Harvey (i.e. Excellence); Steve Ham, Dr. Jason Lisle, and Tim Chaffey (Answers in Genesis); and the entire team at Master Books/New Leaf Publishing.

Special thanks to my wife, Karla, who has been an encourager, soundboard, editor, and stand-in for the skeptic when needed. Special thanks also to Greg Hampson who took considerable care not only to read but meditate upon (in the biblical sense, p. 54) the manuscript. A final special thanks to Dr. J. Budziszewski for critiquing the formative ideas that eventually became this book and for encouraging me to move forward.

CONTENTS

POP CULTURE REFERENCES

Prepare your group to

MEET THE **SKEPTIC**

with

Workbook
$4.99 | 978-0-89051-659-1

Leader Guide
$7.99 | 978-0-89051-667-6

Use this workbook and leader's guide to teach others how to present their faith
in Jesus Christ and defend a biblical worldview with confidence.

WHY THIS BOOK IS DIFFERENT

What is a skeptic? For our purposes, skeptics are people who discard the biblical worldview in favor of other ways to see the world. Some had nonbelieving parents. Some had believing parents who were legalistic. Some have been deceived by false teachers and false religions. Some have been turned off by hypocrites. Some have put their trust in material success and their own abilities. Some have been influenced by skeptical academics and experts. We meet them every day at work, in class, at the gym, and in the grocery store. We are long past the time of dropping a biblical reference into a conversation and expecting its significance to be recognized. Our post-Christian culture requires us to do more remedial work with potential believers in order to make an impact.

Because there are so many diverse ideas out there, we need to cross-train ourselves to be ready for scrutiny and skepticism. But skepticism provides a great opportunity; it gives us a platform to explain why we believe what we believe. It shows us where the need for truth is. Even if we don't get the chance to mention Jesus, that doesn't mean we can't reveal truth that ultimately leads to Him.

Conversations with skeptics can become a game of fetch. A skeptic tosses out a sound-bite objection and the believer tries to retrieve an answer. If the believer is familiar with the objection or happens to have collected some sound bites of his own, he* may offer a specific answer. If he is not familiar with the objection, he may fall back on a "churchism" such as *"God said it. I believe it. That settles it!"* or *"You just have to have faith."*** He may also lunge for a Bible verse, get defensive, try to discredit the skeptic's source, or become too frustrated to say anything.

But even if the believer is able to recall just the right piece of information for a valid answer, where does it get him?

*Masculine pronouns used throughout for brevity.
**My criticism of Christian clichés does not reflect an Emergent Church philosophy that rejects these kinds of responses only to replace them with its own relativistic views (p.72).

The skeptic will just follow it up with another objection, sending the believer scrambling again. This tactic prevents the believer from making a meaningful point and from understanding how the skeptic really sees the world.

Believers get discouraged because they think they must learn an encyclopedia of answers. But trying to memorize a loose collection of answers and then waiting for an objection that matches them is a clumsy way to prepare. Unlike Mormons and Jehovah's Witnesses, who although misinformed undergo extensive training, evangelicals are taught to spread the gospel (evangelize), but many are poorly equipped to pre-evangelize the post-Christian culture. And although there are plenty of great apologetics* resources available, Christians lack a model for how to apply them. We hold the keys, but we don't have a key ring on which to hang them.

Meet the Skeptic addresses this problem. It does not try to be a replacement for conventional apologetics or de-emphasize the need to study specific issues. Rather, it provides believers a mental framework for learning and responding to worldviews rather than objections.

Answering objections should not be our primary concern; we should first recognize and engage the worldviews feeding those objections. The method in this book stresses understanding worldviews as categories. We can do this by identifying the big ideas (herein called "Root Ideas") at the core of a skeptic's objections.

By training you in four basic worldview categories and a few conversational tools, this book will help you become a better critical thinker, articulator, and defender of your biblical worldview. You should not be intimidated or offended by skeptics' objections to the biblical worldview. Objections are opportunities. They reveal a nonbeliever's need for truth, and they challenge us to make our faith relevant.

---

*Giving a reasoned defense of the faith (Phil. 1:7, 1Pet. 3:15)

COLOSSIANS 4:2-6

Devote yourselves to prayer,
being watchful and thankful.

And pray for us, too, that God
may open a door for our message,
so that we may proclaim the mystery
of Christ, for which I am in chains.

Pray that I may proclaim it clearly,
as I should.

Be wise in the way you act
toward outsiders; make the most
of every opportunity.

Let your conversation be always
full of grace, seasoned with salt,
so that you may know how
to answer everyone.

At this point Festus interrupted Paul's defense. "You are out of your mind, Paul!" he shouted. "Your great learning is driving you insane."

"I am not insane, most excellent Festus," Paul replied. "What I am saying is true and reasonable."

Then Agrippa said to Paul, "Do you think that in such a short time you can persuade me to be a Christian?"*

- Acts 26:24-25, 28

1: MAKING YOUR FAITH RELEVANT

My friend: "So, Jesus was born of a virgin?
  C'mon, Bill, you don't really believe that, do you?"
Me: "...err...uh...well, the Bible says..."

This is an excerpt from a conversation I had with a friend back in college. His remark showed that he was already unimpressed with what the Bible had to say, so my desperate lunge for a Bible quote fell on deaf ears. He believed that the Bible was no more authoritative than a supermarket tabloid. He also thought I had inherited my belief system from my parents, that I had accepted it without examination. In one sense, he was right.

Up to this point, my faith was based more on experience (conviction, confession, repentance, forgiveness) than on something concrete. This did not invalidate my faith, but it also did not make it any more accessible for most skeptics. Regarding my friend's objection, I believed in the virgin birth because I believed the Bible, but I wasn't able to share reasons for why the Bible is believable. My beliefs had not encountered much resistance; they had been affirmed by godly family and friends. The only problem was that none of them were around to help. I didn't know how to put spiritual truth in real terms for nonbelievers. It was time for me to take off the training wheels and learn how to explain why I believed what I believed to someone with a different worldview. I needed this experience and others like it to motivate me to become a better student of my faith. What had I really learned from being a Christian since the age of twelve? From Sunday school? From years of sitting in the church pew?

but I'm not a scholar

"In religion and politics people's beliefs and convictions are in almost every case gotten at second-hand, and without examination, from authorities who have not themselves examined the questions at issue but have taken them at second-hand from other non-examiners, whose opinions about them were not worth a brass farthing."[1]

- Mark Twain

Both skeptics and Christians are guilty of not thinking through their beliefs. Clichés and bumper-sticker wisdom are examples of unexamined philosophy that we all fall back on at times. Many skeptics don't know why they believe what they believe and merely parrot the clichés of today's culture with expressions such as: *"All religions are the same"; "Against abortion? Don't have one"; "That's true for you but not true for me"; "Science has disproven the Bible"; and "Christianity is so exclusive!"*

Christians resort to churchisms such as: *"Let go and let God"; "Love the sinner, hate the sin"; "I have Jesus in my heart"; "God said it. I believe it. That settles it!"* As Twain put it, are these responses *"worth a brass farthing"*?

Although being a scholar is not a prerequisite for being an effective believer, we all should be able to explain in basic language how our faith is different and why it makes sense. The term "thinking Christian" should not be an oxymoron.

A potential-believer friend of mine recently made a discouraging observation. He said, *"It's funny, when I ask people who say they are Christians if they believe the Bible is inerrant, many of them say, 'No.' And when I ask Christians who do believe the Bible is inerrant why they believe it, they say something like, 'You just have to have faith.'"*

Would these answers motivate you to learn more about Christianity if you were an unbeliever? Although it's true that "you can't just reason people to Jesus," it is also true that ignorance won't win them over. Reasonable arguments are necessary to raise their interest, give them food for thought, and demonstrate the credibility of Christians and Christianity.

winning and losing

Arthur: "Now stand aside, worthy adversary."
Black Knight: "'Tis but a scratch."
Arthur: "A scratch? Your arm's off!"
Black Knight: "No, it isn't."
Arthur: "Well, what's that then?"(pointing to severed arm)
Black Knight: "I've had worse."[2]
- *Monty Python and the Holy Grail* (1975)

How often after disagreeing with someone have they responded to you with, *"Wow! You got me there...that is truly a convincing argument. I admit I will have to reverse my beliefs on this matter and change the way I live"*? Even if your argument did convince them, are they going to admit it in front of you? Not likely. Everyone has their pride to protect.

If, like me, you are competitive, you need to resist the tendency to try to win the discussion. You could make a great argument and be completely ignored (*"When you tell them all this, they will not listen to you; when you call to them, they will not answer"* [Jer. 7:27]). The important thing is to leave the door open for future conversations. Don't sever the relationship by trying to win. As Christian apologist Ravi Zacharias is fond of saying, *"Once you've cut off a person's nose, there's no point giving him a rose to smell."*[3] The right attitude may earn you another chance later (1 Pet. 3:15).

Understand that our task is not to convert or even to convince them; it is to *communicate truth.* We can't expect logical arguments alone to convert skeptics–only the Holy Spirit can do that. But when challenged, we need to be able to show that the biblical worldview makes sense, and that skepticism is a dead end when it comes to answering life's questions. What the skeptic does with that information is up to him.

Does not the ear test words as the tongue tastes food?

- Job 12:11

2: TEST THEIR WORDS

start with a question

Asking questions before spitting out answers is the key to clarifying language and to moving beyond bumper-sticker reasoning. If the skeptic is noticeably antagonistic, first ask, *"Do you really want an answer?"* If he is just baiting you, there is no need to go any further. But if he is receptive, start with a question such as: *"How so?"; "What do you mean by that?";* or *"What I hear you saying is..."* Here is an example of a conversation my wife had with a gentleman at the gym–we'll call him Jack–who questioned why she was reading a book supporting biblical creation:

> *Jack:* "I believe in evolution. If God had something to do with it, he's not involved now."
> *My wife:* "Why do you think that?"
> *Jack:* "Because if God was involved now, there wouldn't be so much bad stuff."
> *My wife:* "Like what?"
> *Jack:* "...Well, you know, suffering."
> *My wife:* "Do you know someone who is suffering?"
> *Jack:* "Yeah...my wife."

Although the scientific subject matter (creation versus evolution) triggered the conversation, Jack's objection really concerned suffering, not science. He needed to know why God would let anyone suffer.*

listen for RED-FLAG Words

Words can depict reality as it really is or they can twist it. Words shape the culture. An integral tool in this book is the Red-Flag-Words list included in each category. These are words skeptics falsely redefine. For example, if a skeptic said that you were being "intolerant" because you disagreed with

---

*See *Bonus Point I* for a response to this difficult question.

his view, stop there and clarify the meaning of "intolerant" because "to disagree" is not its true meaning (p. 75). When we hear words like this, a mental red flag should go up alerting us that the skeptic is misrepresenting ideas.

Jesus responded to a Red-Flag word when He encountered the rich young man who asked, *"Good teacher, what must I do to inherit eternal life?"* Jesus replied, *"Why do you call me good?"* (Mark 10:17-18). Instead of giving a direct answer, Jesus questioned the young man's understanding of "good" to uncover his motives and assumptions. We can do the same thing. Clarifying the meaning of words alone can defuse many objections.

Words can depict reality as it really is
or they can twist it.

Clarifying the meaning of words alone
can defuse many objections.

"You are bringing some strange ideas to our ears, and we want to know what they mean."

- the Athenian philosophers to Paul, Acts 17:20

3: SPEAK THEIR LANGUAGE

Have you ever described a problem to a mechanic or a computer technician who responded with jargon that was foreign to you? Our answers to skeptics can come across the same way. Sometimes we use words that are misunderstood by the culture or that carry a negative, outdated, or obscure connotation. Here are a few frequently used words and phrases we may need to clarify or to avoid using altogether:

clarify
- "BORN AGAIN"
- "FAITH"
- "IN CHRIST"
- "IN MY HEART"
- "INSPIRED" (Inspiration of Scripture)
- "PERSONAL RELATIONSHIP"
- "SAVED"
- "SIN"

avoid
- "TO ME"
- THEOLOGICAL TERMS
- THE "KING'S ENGLISH"

words to clarify

"BORN AGAIN"

WE SAY: "A person must be *born again* in order to get to heaven."

SKEPTIC HEARS: "A desperate person needs a mystical or emotional experience in order to gain a sense of purpose."

To a skeptic, the term "born again" smacks of irrational, religious fanaticism. The expression, which comes directly from Jesus (John 3:3), will probably be as misunderstood today as it was by Nicodemus. A good explanation for being born again is to say something like this:

"My faith in Christ has changed me. I'm not perfect, but I

desire to do what pleases God instead of what pleases me. I can't work my way to heaven, but I want to be obedient to Christ because He made it possible for me to get there."

"FAITH"

WE SAY: "I have *faith* that Jesus rose from the dead."

SKEPTIC HEARS: "I'll believe anything the Bible says."

The key to explaining true faith is to point out its connection to evidence. Faith is only as good as the object in which it is placed. We need to make clear that real faith is not a feel-good crutch based on wishful thinking. Biblical faith is not blind, flimsy, or afraid of scrutiny. It is not an excuse that fills the gaps in our understanding. Here is the biblical definition of "faith" from Hebrews 11:1 (emphasis added):

Now faith is being <u>sure</u> of what we hope for and <u>certain</u> of what we do not see (NIV).

Now faith is the <u>assurance</u> of things hoped for, the <u>conviction</u> of things not seen (NASB).

Now faith is the <u>substance</u> of things hoped for, the <u>evidence</u> of things not seen (NKJV).

This verse in conjunction with other verses like Romans 1:20 indicates that by testing and investigating what we *can* observe, we can build reasonable confidence about what we *cannot* observe. *Blind* faith is *not* a biblical principle. Consider these passages:

Blind faith is *not* a biblical principle.

Testing and investigation
build an account of credibility
that funds our faith.

- *"Love the Lord your God with all your heart and with all your soul and with all your mind and with all your strength"* (Mark 12:30).

  >> Jesus never asks us to turn off reason when relating to God.

- *"Believe me when I say that I am in the Father and the Father is in me; or at least believe on the evidence of the miracles themselves"* (John 14:11).

  >> It is only logical that nothing short of a miracle is sufficient evidence of the divine. Miracles support Jesus' repeated claims to be God.* (See also Paul's argument in Acts 17:31.)

- "*For since the creation of the world God's invisible qualities– his eternal power and divine nature–have been clearly seen, being understood from what has been made, so that men are without excuse"* (Rom. 1:20).

  >> This verse agrees nicely with scientific inquiry. Based on observation and understanding, not wishful thinking, we can reasonably conclude that the world is no accident.

Here is a simple illustration to describe biblical faith:

Spending Spree

Suppose that whenever I face one of life's difficult situations I go on a shopping spree. I burn up the credit cards on all the toys I want in an attempt to make my life happier. But what if my bank account was empty from the beginning because I never earned the funds to fill it? One day, all my stuff will be repossessed. The lift I felt while "buying" and enjoying my things will evaporate into despair. Similarly, faith without evidence is vulnerable to challenges and unlikely to provide lasting assurance.

Testing and investigation build an account of credibility that funds our faith. Even if we don't know all the evidence behind our faith, it doesn't change the fact that more than enough exists for us and for skeptics to examine if necessary.

*Contrary to many skeptics who deny that Jesus claims this, the scriptural evidence is clear and abundant. See BONUS POINT IV.

"IN CHRIST"

<u>WE SAY</u>: "We can't realize our full potential unless we are growing *in Christ.*"

<u>SKEPTIC THINKS</u>: "Huh?"

The expression "in Christ" is commonly used by believers perhaps because we read it so often in the writings of the apostle Paul. However, it is an odd expression if you didn't grow up in church. The preposition *in* makes it confusing. Suppose Michael Jordan said, *"I was able to fully realize my jump shot <u>in</u> coach Dean Smith."* It sounds a little weird. But that's the way nonbelievers hear us–in secular context, not biblical context. What *in* really means is, *because of* or *through the power of.* So, we can restate our *"in Christ"* comment above as: *"We can't realize our full potential unless we are growing <u>through the power of</u> Christ."* If we say that up front, we will sound a little more accessible.

"IN MY HEART"

<u>WE SAY</u>: "I know *in my heart* the Bible is true."

<u>SKEPTIC HEARS</u>: "It makes me feel good to believe the Bible is true."

"In my heart" is a weak and subjective attempt to authenticate any objective truth. *"I know in my heart that I didn't overdraw my bank account"* or *"I know in my heart that I wasn't speeding"* carries little weight with the bank or with a police officer, respectively. Using it with a skeptic who wants evidence of your beliefs will result in eye-rolling. In biblical times, the heart referred to the decision-making center of one's being– the mind, will, and emotions.[1] But in today's culture, the heart represents desires and feelings. In this context, "in my heart" sounds like a purely emotional way of knowing. There is so much objective evidence consistent with our faith, it is an insult to relegate its truth to the realm of feelings. If a skeptic asks why you believe in the Bible or Christianity, give him solid answers.

Nonbelievers hear us in secular context,
not biblical context.

"INSPIRED"

WE SAY: "The Bible is a book *inspired* by the Holy Spirit."

SKEPTIC HEARS: "Emotional experiences and delusions about God motivated men to write the Bible."

Being inspired to play the guitar after listening to Jimi Hendrix or being inspired to play golf after watching Tiger Woods is not what we mean when we say that the Bible is inspired by the Holy Spirit. This kind of inspiration is more like *motivation.*

The Bible's authors were not merely motivated to write down thoughts and experiences. Second Peter 1:20-21 says, *"Above all, you must understand that no prophecy of Scripture came about by the prophet's own interpretation. For prophecy never had its origin in the will of man, but men spoke from God as they were <u>carried along</u> by the Holy Spirit."* The Greek verb for "carried along," *pheromenoi,* is the same word used in Acts 27:15, *"The ship was caught by the storm and could not head into the wind; so <u>we gave way to it</u> and were <u>driven along</u>."*[2] The idea is that the Bible writers were driven by and gave way to the Holy Spirit's power but maintained their own style and personality in their writing.

"PERSONAL RELATIONSHIP"

WE SAY: "I have a *personal relationship* with Jesus Christ."

SKEPTIC HEARS: "God is my co-pilot."

A skeptic in our relativistic culture needs to understand that "personal relationship" does not mean that our connection to Jesus is dictated by our self-serving preferences or by what makes us comfortable. At times, even close friends such as Peter were made very uncomfortable by Jesus (*"When Simon*

Peter saw this, he fell at Jesus' knees and said, 'Go away from me, Lord; I am a sinful man!'" [Luke 5:8]). "Personal relationship" means that each person who has acknowledged Jesus as his Savior can approach Him *without an intermediary* for guidance, consolation, forgiveness, etc.

"SAVED"

WE SAY: "You must be *saved* in order to enter heaven."

SKEPTIC THINKS: "Saved from what?"

It might be disconcerting for some skeptics to understand that the first threat to sinful human beings is not hell or Satan, but God Himself. Because God is holy (p. 52) and we are not, we must be saved both *from* His wrath and *by* Him. The Bible uses a couple of memorable metaphors for salvation that are easy to explain to non-believers. The first depicts removal of sin as a change of clothing. In one symbolic vision, a priest wearing filthy clothes representing Israel is given clean clothes and told that his sin is taken away (Zec. 3:3-5). Again, in Matthew 22, Jesus tells a parable in which a king (God) invites people off the street (Gentiles/sinners) to His son's (Jesus') wedding banquet. But when He discovers that some are wearing their own clothes (self-righteousness) instead of the wedding clothes He has provided (perfect righteousness)– a serious insult–He has them thrown out into the night.

The second metaphor illustrates salvation in book-keeping terms. In His model prayer, Jesus says to ask God to "forgive us our *debts*" (Matt. 6:12). Paul explains that our faith (not our works) will be *credited* as righteousness (Rom. 4:1-5) and that *"the wages of sin is death, but the gift of God is eternal life"* (Rom. 6:23).

We are ready to be saved only when we recognize how spiritually needy we are. If we rely on our own dirty hands and empty spiritual pockets for salvation, we reject the cleansing and payment from the only One who can provide it.

"SIN"

<u>WE SAY</u>: "Everyone is guilty of *sin*."

<u>SKEPTIC HEARS</u>: "Really bad people like Hitler are going to hell."

For most skeptics, nothing short of extreme violence (or the cardinal sin of *intolerance,* p. 75) should be considered sin. That is why they may get defensive if you suggest they are sinful. It is important to explain that everyone is guilty of sin (Rom. 3:10-12; 8:6-8; Col. 1:21) because we are naturally inclined to settle for our own standards instead of aiming for God's perfect standards (Ten Commandments, Sermon on the Mount, James 2:10, etc.). Very simply, sin is falling short of God's standards by pleasing the self rather than pleasing God.

words not to use
"TO ME"

This may seem like an insignificant phrase, but look at this example from an interview in *USA Today* with star comedic actor Jim Carrey (emphasis added):

> *"I discovered a new thing in the Lord's Prayer that kind of hit me," Carrey says. "'On earth as it is heaven' <u>to me</u> means whatever you take out into the world is what you're going to draw out. Like those days when you're all yang and no yin, and you're fighting with people inside, and you can't calm yourself down, and suddenly you're pulled over by the cops. Everything goes wrong in the same day because you created it."*

> *"So, if you get heaven within you, it'll be all around you. If hell is within you, it'll be all around you. It's always created here first."[3]*

By using the "to me" philosophy, Jim Carrey stands the Lord's Prayer on its head. He completely reverses the

Never qualify the meaning of
a Bible verse by using "to me."

point of the prayer which is to model for us how to seek the will of God in heaven *above*–not "heaven within"–to determine our direction here on earth.

Never qualify the meaning of a Bible verse by using "to me." Our personal take on a Bible passage is irrelevant. Personalizing a passage only feeds our relativistic culture. Instead say, *"According to the context of the passage/book, this verse means..."*

THEOLOGICAL TERMS

If you are familiar with some theological terms, explain them in everyday language:

Justification: "I am considered righteous in God's eyes even though I didn't do anything to earn it."

Sanctification: "God transforms my will so that I can live more righteously."

Propitiation: "Jesus' sacrifice on the cross for us satisfied God's judgment against our sinfulness (if we accept it)."

Imputation: "Jesus' righteousness is credited to me, and my sinfulness is credited to Him."

THE KING'S ENGLISH

The King James Version is a good Bible translation, but King James vernacular is not a particularly effective way to communicate with the current culture. Filter these kinds of expressions:

Abide: "You're *abiding* in your sin."
>> Instead say, "We get comfortable doing what pleases us instead of what pleases God."

Manifest: "The works of God were made *manifest* in Jesus."
>> Instead say, "Jesus perfectly embodied the work and character of God."

use illustrations

One of the best ways to speak in a way that anyone can understand is to give an illustration. Illustrations can make your explanations more concrete. They can be word pictures (such as *Spending Spree*, p.13), short stories, or examples that you think relate to the skeptic's interests, background, or current situation. In the Root Idea chapter of each category, you will find a few effective illustrations to use.

All the Athenians and the foreigners who lived there spent their time doing nothing but talking about and listening to the latest ideas.

- Acts 17:21

DON'T PULL THE WEEDS

4: THE 4 KINDS OF SKEPTICISM

Generally speaking, a person's total worldview consists of how he sees the world in three broad categories: SPIRITUAL, MORAL, and SCIENTIFIC. These three areas represent life's big questions such as: *What happens after we die?* (Spiritual); *Are right and wrong absolute?* (Moral); *How did life come about?* (Scientific), etc. So SPIRITUAL, MORAL, and SCIENTIFIC skepticism are three of the four kinds of skepticism you can expect when you engage a skeptic.

The fourth kind is *BIBLICAL*. The Bible is the lens through which believers view the other three categories. Although skeptics don't use the Bible to shape their worldview or to guide their life, most will give an opinion about it when given the opportunity. Therefore, when we engage skeptics we bring a biblical worldview into the conversation and create the possibility that it will be questioned.

Keep in mind that the point of the categories is not to label or categorize *people**, but rather to make us aware of what kind of *skepticism* they are expressing at the time, and therefore, what kind of conversation we are engaging.

dig up the Root Ideas not the weeds

For each of the four kinds of skepticism, there is a Root Idea that feeds the various objections within that category. What we're calling the Root Idea is the false premise. A false premise feeds objections like a root feeds a weed. Pulling a dandelion will only dislodge its feathery seeds and leave the root eventually creating more dandelions. Similarly, if we respond to each objection a skeptic raises, he just raises another one to take its place. Our goal is to dig up Root Ideas not debate the many objections (pull up the weeds) growing out of them.

For example, suppose a skeptic says the History Channel showed archaeological proof of "missing books" of

---

*It goes without saying that people are complicated. A skeptic could express ideas belonging to any one or all four of the categories.

the Bible. If you knew about this particular finding you could debate its authenticity, or you could question a bias by the History Channel. But these options would create a surface-level ping-pong match. Instead, question the likely Root Idea which is, *"The Bible is man-made"* (p. 36) to get to a more meaningful level of his worldview.

The following is a brief description of each kind of skepticism, its Root Idea, and a Probing Question to expose it:

SPIRITUAL

You've encountered a SPIRITUAL objection if it involves:
• Questions about God
• Other religions/cults
• The afterlife
• The supernatural

Sample objections:
   "People can get to heaven by many paths."
   "Your imagination creates your destiny."
   "Meditation brings me closer to enlightenment."

The Root Idea behind most SPIRITUAL objections is:
"Good works get you heaven."

A Probing Question to ask is:
"How good is good enough (to get you to heaven)?"

MORAL

You've encountered a MORAL objection if it involves:
• Truth
• Peace (at the expense of truth)
• Fairness/justice
• Autonomy (self-rule)
• God's justice/the Bible's fairness
• Sex (unmarried sex, homosexuality, abortion)
• War (justified or not?)
• "Art" (as a label to protect all forms of expression)

Sample objections:

"How can you say your values are better than someone else's?"

"There are no moral absolutes."

"How could a good God send anyone to hell?"

The Root Idea behind most MORAL objections is:

"People should decide for themselves what is right or wrong."

A Probing Question to ask is:

"What is your standard for right and wrong?"

SCIENTIFIC

You've encountered a SCIENTIFIC objection if it involves:

• Divorcing reason from faith
• The universe (Big Bang, etc.)
• Evolution

Sample objections:

"God is an irrational crutch people use to explain things they don't understand."

"The Big Bang started the universe." ("Creation in six days is a nice story for kids.")

"There are so many similarities between humans and apes...it's easy to see that we evolved."

The Root Idea behind most SCIENTIFIC objections is:

"The natural world is all that there is."

(Nature can do godlike things.)

A Probing Question to ask is:

"How much faith is required for that belief?"

BIBLICAL

You've encountered a BIBLICAL objection if it involves:

• The Bible's authority
• The Bible's reliability
• The Bible's relevance

Sample objections:

"The Bible authors were just men with their own biases."

"We can't trust the Bible because it has been corrupted by many years of copying and translation."

"The Bible no longer applies to our modern world."

The Root Idea behind most BIBLICAL objections is:

"The Bible is man-made."

(It originated with man rather than God.)

A Probing Question to ask is:

"If God gave us a book, how would we know it really came from Him?"

Specific questions about Bible passages are not included in the BIBLICAL category. One reason is that many skeptics already have a tainted view of the Bible before they read any of it. If you quote from it to prove a point, they have no reason to believe that it is any more authoritative than any other book. The BIBLICAL category is set up to reshape their understanding of its authority, reliability, and relevance before debating its content.

The second reason specific questions about Bible passages are not included in the model is that they should be somewhat covered by our DAILY STUDY OF THE BIBLE, not by additional techniques such as those described in this book. If you encounter someone who sincerely wants an explanation of a particular passage (not just using the Bible as a front for another kind of objection), set aside this model, let the Bible speak for itself, and be ready to put it in context for them. See *BONUS POINT II* for five areas of the Bible to study to prepare for the most common questions.

THE **MEET-THE-SKEPTIC MODEL** OVERVIEW

SPIRITUAL **MORAL** **SCIENTIFIC** **BIBLICAL**

1) **REMEMBER 4 CATEGORIES**

2) **CLARIFY WORDS**
   - Clarify the objection *(How so?, etc.)*
   - Define Red-Flag words

3) **DIG UP ROOT IDEAS**
   - Ask Probing Questions

You may or may not be able to do all of the above in one conversation, but doing any one of them will bring the exchange to a meaningful level much quicker than playing ping-pong with their objection.

Now let's look at the first Root Idea beginning with the SPIRITUAL category.

SPIRITUAL SKEPTICISM

SPIRITUAL SKEPTICISM IN A NUTSHELL

Spirituality fails as a worldview because it is self-defeating; people trust their own flawed works as the means to reach a state of perfection and perfect peace. People want the freedom to get to heaven their own way. This is the "wide gate" leading to destruction that Jesus warns about (Matt. 7:13-14). The wide gate consists of as many techniques for climbing the stairway to heaven as there are people to imagine them.

But for the freedom gained by climbing toward heaven in one's own way, there is the unending burden of the climb itself. Natural man would rather saddle himself with trying to live up to spiritual laws instead of believing that a perfect Savior has already done this on his behalf. Spirituality provides a temporary, feel-good sense of accomplishment, but it is a futile, self-serving attempt at salvation. The individual has only himself to thank for his efforts, but also only himself to blame when he realizes they aren't good enough.

Romans 10:9 offers the liberation spirituality can not: *"That if you confess with your mouth, 'Jesus is Lord,' and believe in your heart that God raised him from the dead, you will be saved."* And in Galatians 3:2-3, Paul criticizes the people for reverting to laws and works to save themselves: *"I would like to learn just one thing from you: Did you receive the Spirit by observing the law, or by believing what you heard? Are you so foolish? After beginning with the Spirit, are you now trying to attain your goal by human effort?"*

This may sound like easy believism to some, but it is the "narrow gate" that few find. If it is so easy to merely believe, why aren't more able to do it? Surrendering self-rule is the most difficult thing for mankind to do. Only in Christianity does one get to heaven by grace, not works. Doesn't that alone make it worth investigating?

"For countless ages, a goal of religion has been the salvage of the human spirit. Man has tried by many practices to find the pathway to salvation. He has held the imperishable hope that someday in some way he would be free."

- L. Ron Hubbard, Founder, Church of Scientology[1]

5: THE SPIRITUAL ROOT IDEA

SPIRITUAL objections involve:
• Questions about God
• Other religions/cults
• The afterlife
• The supernatural

sample objections:

"People can get to heaven by many paths."
"Our words and thoughts shape our reality."
"Meditation brings me closer to enlightenment."

Aside from his many bizarre views, I think L. Ron Hubbard was right in the quote at left. He identifies the primary reason people turn to religion and spirituality: to be set free from the problems of our mortal world. The Bible explains why man has this internal drive for spiritual freedom. Ecclesiastes 3:11 says, *"He has made everything beautiful in its time. He has also set eternity in the hearts of men; yet they cannot fathom what God has done from beginning to end."* Further, Romans 1 and 2 explain that the moral law inside us and the natural world around us point to a Creator beyond us.

Religion and spirituality are man's attempt to restore the soul and to reach a Creator or ultimate reality. The vast majority of the world's population and about 90 percent of Americans claim a belief in God or a higher power.[2] And although the many belief systems disagree about what to do to reach Him/Her/It, the one belief they all share—except for Christianity—is that man must *do* something.

dressing for heaven

Religion and *spirituality* are two approaches to spiritual freedom/perfection. Think of religion as a formal dress code for heaven (or whatever final destination is in view). One must clothe one's self in good works and satisfy established ordinances to be admitted to a heavenly afterlife. Islam's dress code is the Five Pillars (profession of faith, ritual prayer, alms-giving, fasting, pilgrimage).[3] Jehovah's Witnesses have four implicit essentials (accurate knowledge, avoiding debauchery, Watchtower membership, proselytism).[4] Mormonism requires numerous works and fulfillment of ordinances to reach tiered levels of eternal glory (Telestial Kingdom, Terrestrial Kingdom, Celestial Kingdom). Buddhism prescribes the Four Noble Truths, the Eightfold Path, avoidance of the Four States of Woe, the Three Scourges, Eight Wrong Circumstances, Four Deficiencies, and on and on.[5]

If religion is a formal dress code, then spirituality is a T-shirt. Spirituality is casual, customized, and likely to be in flux depending on the individual's changing preferences during his independent journey to enlightenment. Spirituality allows the individual to set the rules in which the deity of his choice will operate. Personal experience and lone discovery supersede the doctrines of "organized religion" (p. 55). This view has been propagated by books such as William P. Young's wildly popular and doctrinally challenged *The Shack,* which depicts a God who seems more tailored to the needs of the main character than to the Bible.*

Whether the approach is formal, established religion or casual, customized spirituality, the critical concept linking all spiritual beliefs other than Christianity is *spiritual perfection through works.* Therefore, the Root Idea of SPIRITUAL objections is:

"Good works get you heaven."

But aren't works a part of Christianity too? Yes, but there is a huge difference. Obeying the Ten Commandments and displaying the fruit of the Spirit (Galatians 5: love, joy, peace, patience, kindness, etc.) are not formulas for reaching God, but are instead responses to God having reached us. Before God can have fellowship with us, we must admit that

*Although written in a Christian framework, *The Shack* departs severely from fundamental Christian doctrine concerning the nature of God. Without right doctrine, the God with whom we're seeking relationship is one of our own making.

Religion

Spirituality

Obeying the Ten Commandments
and displaying the fruit of the Spirit
are not formulas for reaching God,
but are instead responses to
God having reached us.

we are morally unfit to attain perfection ourselves. Until we recognize that our works are "filthy rags" (Isa. 64:6), we can never be clothed in the righteousness only Christ can provide.

digging up the SPIRITUAL Root Idea

If the afterlife is a perfected existence, why would any standard short of perfection be good enough to get us there (*basically good,* p. 50)? If "basically good" people are the kind who will populate heaven, how will heaven be much different than our current fallen world? Yet all religious and spiritual systems other than Christianity maintain that the works of "basically good" people will get them to a heaven-like place. The trouble is they offer no assurance of what qualifies as good enough. The Probing Question we should ask skeptics who pose spiritual objections is:

"How good is good enough (to get you to heaven)?"

Religion and spirituality make two significant errors: they exaggerate the character of man and/or diminish the nature of God. These two errors put spiritual skeptics in a corner. They must either: 1) believe that man can fulfill the perfect standards of God (the only standards worthy of a true God); or 2) believe in a god who has compromised standards (i.e., "basically good" is good enough for him).

In the Bible, God leaves no doubt about His standards compared to man's: *"...You thought I was altogether like you. But I will rebuke you and accuse you to your face."* (Ps. 50:21); *"As the heavens are higher than the earth, so are my ways higher than your ways and my thoughts than your thoughts"* (Isa. 55:9).

Only in Christianity is God's perfect holiness and humanity's fallenness resolved without diminishing either. Because God is holy and we're not, God's justice and mercy toward us must be satisfied by the only known source of perfection, God Himself. Jesus' perfect life and death on our behalf accomplishes this because He is the only one qualified.

In fact, He is the only one who claims to qualify–neither Buddha, Muhammad, nor any other founder of a major religion claimed to be a Savior but merely an example or prophet.

SPIRITUAL illustrations

The following three illustrations might help you explain the uniqueness of Christianity and the flawed philosophy of doing good works to attain salvation:

#1. Basically Good?

To bring the point home to the skeptic that "basically good" really isn't good enough, tailor questions to his interests or vocation such as the ones listed below:

• "Is a basically good student accepted into medical school?"
• "Is a basically good programmer hired by Bill Gates?"
• "Is a basically good businessman hired by Donald Trump?"
• "Is a basically good computer artist hired by George Lucas?"
• "Does a basically good football player make the NFL?"

>> Then why would a basically good person be allowed into the presence of a perfect, holy God?"

#2. Dividing Line

If the skeptic claims that all religions are basically the same or that they all lead to the same place, use the following illustration:

Draw a line dividing a piece of paper in half. On one side write the heading, "RELIGION," and under it write, "saved by works" and "Jesus was a good teacher." On the other side write, "CHRISTIANITY," and under it write, "saved by grace" and "Jesus is God."

The mantra, "All religions are basically the same," is partially true. What ties them all together is works-based salvation and the claim that Jesus is something less than God.[6] But Christianity is not a religion in this sense. It is radically different from all other religions in a number of ways*, but the subordinate role of works and the divinity of Jesus are two major differences that illustrate the distinction quickly and clearly. To say that all religions are the same is an insult to not only Christianity but also other major religions because none of them say that either.

Ask the skeptic why he shouldn't at least consider the one faith system that is unique—the only one that both satisfies the standards of a perfect God and shows mercy to man's flawed character. Shouldn't Christianity be considered, if for no other reason, because its method of salvation is unlike any other belief system?

RELIGION	CHRISTIANITY
1. SAVED BY WORKS	1. SAVED BY GRACE THROUGH FAITH
2. JESUS WAS A GOOD MAN, WISE TEACHER, ETC.	2. JESUS WAS/IS GOD

#3. Eye Surgery

Can man's own flawed mind and corrupt nature also be the vehicles for his enlightenment (p. 50)? Ask the skeptic, *"If you were partially blind, would you be able to operate on your own eyes and correct your sight?"* Since man is a product of his broken world, his ideas about how to fix himself and his ability to do so are also broken.

---

*Five other big differences are: the nature of God, the nature of man, sin, salvation, and creation.

Oprah:
"When you connected to the higher Self ...knowing that you can do anything that you want to do–is it what other people describe as being 'born again'?"

Shirley MacLaine (nodding):
"Yes, probably."

-*The Oprah Winfrey Show* [1]

6: SPIRITUAL RED-FLAG WORDS

The language of "spiritual" or "religious" people can be confusing. They may use Christian-sounding terms but pour new meanings into them. "Born again" takes on an entirely different meaning than Jesus intended in the mouths of Oprah and Shirley MacLaine–both advocates of do-it-yourself spirituality. Some formal religions create the same confusion. For example, when Mormons say they "accept Christ as their savior," it sounds authentically Christian until you recognize that they have a completely different understanding of who Jesus is and of what salvation means.*

About 76 percent of Americans claim to be Christians, but *only 9 percent* have a biblical worldview.[2,3] So it is common to hear Americans mixing and matching assorted spiritual terms to describe their beliefs: meditation = prayer; enlightenment = salvation; basically good = holy; etc.

Here we will look at a few key terms that express the flawed Root Idea that is common to both religion and spirituality:

- "BASICALLY GOOD"
- "ENLIGHTENED (SELF-ACTUALIZED)"
- "HEAVEN"
- "HOLY"
- "KARMA"
- "MEDITATION"
- "ORGANIZED RELIGION"

*For Mormons, salvation means *exaltation* to the highest level of the Celestial Kingdom which requires doing works and following ordinances prescribed by the Mormon church *in addition to* Jesus' sacrifice.

"BASICALLY GOOD"

<u>SKEPTIC'S MEANING</u>

Doing more good deeds than bad deeds

Do basically good people go to heaven? Would a good God send anyone to hell? When skeptics appeal to God's goodness, they condemn themselves. God's standard is perfect righteousness, not mere human goodness. Most people consider themselves basically good, but this is a loose standard that excuses much of their compromised behavior. If God is perfectly just, He must judge the things we overlook. God demands justice (payment) for sin, but He also provides the payment (righteousness via Jesus). When skeptics reject that payment and rely on their own human standard of goodness, God can only judge them accordingly (Ps. 51:5; Rom. 3:10-12, 23; Mark 10:18).

"ENLIGHTENED (SELF-ACTUALIZED)"

<u>SKEPTIC'S MEANING</u>

Divine self-mastery;[4] finding reality from within

Mark Victor Hansen, co-author of the best-selling *Chicken Soup for the Soul*, says this:

> In India, guru means "self-realized being." To be self-actualized means divine self-mastery–you literally learn how to tell your thinking mind how to think and your feeling mind how to feel, so you pre-ordain your destiny. If all life is imaginal, meaning imagination creates your reality (which I believe), then you want to have an imagination that is under your control.[5]

So the flawed mind is the vehicle for becoming an enlightened mind? In the 2001 film, *A Beautiful Mind*, mathematical genius and schizophrenic John Nash, played by Russell Crowe, is told by his psychiatrist that he can not reason his way out of his condition as if it were a math problem.

In denial of this fact, Nash responds in frustration, *"Why not? Why can't I?"* The doctor replies, *"Because your mind is where the problem is in the first place."*[6]

This exchange sums up the human spiritual condition; man cannot enlighten himself because his nature is where the problem is. (*The heart is deceitful above all things and beyond cure. Who can understand it?* [Jer. 17:9].) Hansen would probably say that one needs a guide or guru to show the way, but how did the guru get beyond his own flawed nature? Is he divine? If man is really divine and only needs to re-recognize his divinity, how did he lose touch with it in the first place? If the divine can be corrupted, is it really divine?

The innate desire to please the self (sin) eventually overcomes man's noble motivations, no matter how many external rules are in place or gurus are employed to prevent it. Only a truly divine source beyond man can provide enlightenment (*Whom did the Lord consult to enlighten him, and who taught him the right way?* [Isa. 40:14]).

"HEAVEN"

SKEPTIC'S MEANING

The place all good people go after they die to have an eternally good time

The key element missing from flawed ideas of heaven is *love*. If love is the highest ethic, shouldn't it be involved in reaching the highest place? Partying with periodic rests upon a cloud (secular Western heaven); "becoming one" with an impersonal, eternal force (Eastern mystical heaven); or spending eternity with 70 virgins (Islamic jihad heaven); have nothing to do with love, but are based on self reward.

Heaven is a place of joy, beauty, peace, and a sinless life (Rev. 21-22). But all of these benefits, although spectacular, will be secondary to our fellowship with and worship of Christ in response to His love and sacrifice for us (John 14:3, Rev. 7:9-12).

"HOLY"

SKEPTIC'S MEANING

Something that has a lot of religious tradition associated with it

From a human perspective, God's holiness is both His greatest and most terrifying attribute. Holy means "marked off" (*qadash* [Heb.])[7] or "set apart" (*hagios* [Gr.])[8] The paradox skeptics miss about God's holiness is that it repels us from Him while being the only thing able to reconnect us to Him. For example, His holiness made Isaiah (Isa. 6:5) and David (2 Sam. 6:9) realize how vulnerable they were in God's presence. Yet it is only because holiness can be transferred via Jesus (Rom. 3:22) and applied via the Holy Spirit (John 16:13) that we can be saved from ruin and have fellowship with God. C. S. Lewis describes the situation this way:

> The Christian religion is, in the long run, a thing of unspeakable comfort. But it does not begin in comfort; it begins in the dismay I have been describing, and it is no use at all trying to go on to that comfort without first going through that dismay.[9]

"KARMA"

SKEPTIC'S MEANING

My good deeds will return to me. I create my own reality.

The Westernized idea of karma has been packaged for popular consumption by Hollywood stars such as Shirley MacLaine and Richard Gere. Being "basically good" is often associated with the idea of karma: doing good will result in good coming back to you either in this life or in the next (i.e., paying it forward). However, many fail to see the mercilessness of karma, which requires endless rebirths without any assurance of freedom. One is enslaved by a perpetual cycle of his own works. Even worse, karma perpetuates the presence of evil

The paradox skeptics miss about God's
holiness is that it repels us from Him
while being the one thing
able to reconnect us to Him.

because one who does evil in this life must be cursed by it in the next.

This endless cycle of suffering is a poor substitute for the mercy and assurance Christ offers: *"So if the Son sets you free, you will be free indeed"* (John 8:36) and *"I am the gate; whoever enters through me will be saved. He will come in and go out, and find pasture"* (John 10:9).

"MEDITATION"
SKEPTIC'S MEANING
Finding a frame of mind to become one with the universe; finding one's inner voice

Mystical meditation and Bible-based prayer are very different. Meditation is passive; prayer is active. Meditation focuses on emptying the mind; prayer requires activating it. (*"So what shall I do? I will pray with my spirit, but I will also pray with my mind; I will sing with my spirit, but I will also sing with my mind"* [1 Cor. 14:15]). Meditation seeks a connection to an impersonal force; prayer seeks a relationship with a personal being.

The Bible directs us to meditate, but there is always an object of our meditation. We are to meditate on God's law (Josh. 1:8), His unfailing love (Ps. 48:9), His mighty deeds (Ps. 77:12), His precepts and ways (Ps. 119:15), His decrees (Ps. 119:23), His wonders (Ps. 119:27), His statutes (Ps. 119:99), His promises (Ps. 119:148), and numerous other things.

"ORGANIZED RELIGION"

<u>SKEPTIC'S MEANING</u>

A narrow, dogmatic, hypocritical belief system

"I took God out of the box because I grew up in the Baptist Church and there were rules, belief systems, and doctrines... God is a feeling experience, not a believing experience. If God for you is still about a belief, it's not truly God."

- Oprah Winfrey, echoing the philosophy of Eckhart Tolle's *A New Earth*[10]

      Maybe the most common reason people give for avoiding organized religion is that it has "too many hypocrites." There are plenty of genuine Christians out there, but even if all of them were hypocrites, the person to whom the skeptic must trust for salvation is not a Christian, it is Christ.

      But the real hindrance for spiritual skeptics to organized religion is not hypocrites but *authority*. Personal experience and discovery are their primary source of authority. Organized religion challenges this authority and restricts their freedom of expression. Oprah states this issue well; she needed to take God *"out of the box."* The *"rules...belief systems...and doctrines"* were a problem for her. She rejected organized religion because it required adherence to a set of beliefs that didn't match her experience. But customized spirituality offers her and others like her the freedom to assemble their own eclectic, usually contradictory, beliefs. The trade-off is that there is no accountability and thus, no true growth.

MORAL SKEPTICISM

MORAL SKEPTICISM IN A NUTSHELL

Moral relativism is a slippery worldview. It is blatantly self-defeating yet alarmingly popular because it sounds so tolerant and inclusive. Relativists want to liberate the world of moral absolutes they believe inhibit personal freedom and expression, yet they advance their own subjective views as absolute standards.

It takes practice to recognize the convoluted language relativists use. They preach against absolutes and judgments but they must use absolutes and judgments to determine that not using them is better. Therefore, the best defense against relativistic language is to turn it on itself. Once the language is exposed, the ideas evaporate and unless absolute truth is recognized, emotionalism will carry their argument. This means we must learn to respond with clarity and grace, not our own emotionalism.

Finally, relativists fail to see that relativism is enslaving, not liberating. If everyone decides for themselves what is right or wrong, standards will eventually conflict and chaos will ensue. If all standards are presumably equal, who then decides what is right? The only alternative is that those with the most *power* will decide. A relativistic world is ultimately governed by one absolute principle–*might* determines *right*. This means relativism leads to a society that is the opposite of the liberated world relativists imagine.

"All we are saying, is give peace a chance."

- John Lennon[1]

7: THE MORAL ROOT IDEA

MORAL objections involve:
- Truth
- Peace (at the expense of truth)
- Fairness/justice
- Autonomy (self-rule)
- God's justice/the Bible's fairness
- Sex (unmarried sex, homosexuality, abortion)
- War (justified or not?)
- "Art" (as a label to protect all forms of expression)

sample objections:

"How can you say your values are better than someone else's?"
"There are no moral absolutes."
"How could a good God send anyone to hell?"

A big reason people gravitate toward moral relativism is that it appears to promote peace and brotherly love. It is the worldview behind the ubiquitous "COEXIST" bumper stickers whose real message is not that all religions should just get along, but that they are all equally true–an impossibility.* Relativism allows an individual to avoid moral judgments. One can appear thoughtful, nonjudgmental, and neutral by saying that right and wrong are things people should decide for themselves (although this is not neutral either; see *should,* p. 82). Conversely, if one holds unbending, absolute truths (Jesus is the only way; marriage is between a man and a woman; a "choice" is really a baby; etc.), he is considered a divisive enemy of peace. But this means that Jesus, the Prince of Peace, is also an enemy of peace because He claimed to embody *the* truth.

Jesus brought peace between God and man (1Tim. 2:5) and taught peace between man and man, but not at the expense of truth. He equated Himself with truth and claimed to

---

*The Law of Non-contradiction says that two opposing statements can not both be true at the same time and in the same sense. Major religions contradict each other at every turn. They all can be wrong, but they all can not be right.

Jesus brought peace and taught peace,
but not at the expense of truth.

be *the* way to God (John 14:6). He even declared that His identity would bring division between members of the same family (Matt. 10:32-37; Luke 12:51-53). This is a hard teaching, but truth often involves making a hard decision and choosing a side–something relativists try to avoid. Let's look at how this moral ambiguity shows up in a famous blockbuster film.

which side is the Dark Side?

Palpatine: "Anakin, search your feelings."

Anakin: "The Jedi use their power for good."

Palpatine: "Good is a point of view, Anakin."

Anakin: "The Sith rely on their passion for their strength.
  They think inwards only about themselves."

Palpatine: "And the Jedi don't?"

Anakin: "If you're not with me, you're my enemy."

Obi-Wan: "Only a Sith Lord deals in absolutes.
  I will do what I must...Anakin, Chancellor Palpatine is evil."

Anakin: "From the Jedi point of view!
  From my point of view, the Jedi are evil."

- *Star Wars: Episode III - Revenge of the Sith* (2005)[2]

When I first saw *Revenge of the Sith* in the theater with my wife and some friends, we got a good laugh out of this kind of dialogue. In the midst of trying to be profound through his characters, George Lucas never realizes the absurdity of the supposed wisdom he imparts.

Anakin's (a.k.a. Darth Vader's) evil mentor, Palpatine, sounds like a moral relativist. His proverb, *"Good is a point of view, Anakin,"* is the definition of moral relativism. But does he really believe this? If he did, he wouldn't be grooming Anakin to destroy his Jedi enemies. Instead, he would just say, *"Good is a point of view, Anakin. Jedi ideas are just as good as ours, so let's just all get along."* But that wouldn't make for a very interesting six-part epic, would it? Anakin, like his master, Palpatine, speaks relativism (*"From my point of view, the Jedi are evil"*), but reveals that he really lives by absolutes when he says to Obi-Wan, *"If you're not with me, you're my enemy."*

But it is not only the *Star Wars* villains who contradict themselves; so do the heroes. The samurai-like Jedi represented by Obi-Wan (and Yoda) are Lucas's moral voice for the *Star Wars* films. Through Obi-Wan, Lucas lectures us about the dangers of the Sith's black-and-white, intolerant, absolutist views. In other words, Lucas frames absolute truth as being dangerously extremist. The irony is that through Obi-Wan he unwittingly exposes the absurdity of moral relativism. Consider this classic pair of self-defeating statements: Obi-Wan says, *"Only a Sith Lord deals in absolutes"* but then says, *"Anakin, Chancellor Palpatine is evil."* (I wanted to yell at the screen, "ISN'T THAT AN ABSOLUTE??!!")

Note that feelings dictate absolutes in the *Star Wars* films just as they often do for moral relativists in real life. Palpatine's advice, *"Anakin, search your feelings"* and Obi-Wan's advice in the original *Star Wars*, *"Trust your feelings, Luke"* are two examples. Unfortunately, the shifting nature of feelings make them an unreliable way to navigate through life.

George Lucas does offer us wisdom, but not the kind he intends. He gives us a vivid picture of why relativism doesn't work. In a sci-fi epic, you can suspend the laws of physics, but you still can't suspend absolute truth. One must use an absolute in order to deny an absolute (e.g., "There are no absolutes!")–no matter how tolerant or inclusive one claims to be.

There is no such thing as a pure relativist, only those who pose as relativists in order to sound morally superior or politically correct. Even people who claim to be relativists must use absolutes (i.e., fixed standards) to determine that relativism is better than absolutism.

the authority of relativism

Unfortunately, relativism's power is not just limited to the Hollywood big screen. Its authority has grown in part through political leaders who espouse it and the postmodern culture to whom they appeal. Relativism is particularly seductive because it hides in plain sight. It seems tolerant, inclusive, and

There is no such thing as a pure relativist,
only those who pose as relativists
in order to sound morally superior
or politically correct.

plays to the public's emotions and sense of morality, but its inherent self-defeating nature slips by unnoticed. During the 2008 presidential campaign, Barack Obama expressed relativism persuasively and routinely. The following interview excerpt (emphasis added) is one example:

> I think that the president has come to approach the problems we face in very _ideological, absolutist_ terms ...And I think that has been _a mistake_. I think that the American people are historically a nonideological people. I think when we operate on the basis of _common sense and pragmatism_, we end up with better outcomes ...it seems as if the president has only one _narrow_ approach and is not taking in the advice and dissenting views that might make for better proposals.[3]

In attempting to appear above the fray, Obama is probably unaware of his statements' self-defeating nature. He is seduced by relativism's appeal as are many who hear this kind of presentation. An inherent problem with relativism is that regardless of the speaker's intent, it is naturally misleading. Obama's remarks criticize ideology while at the same time promoting the ideology of _"common sense and pragmatism."_* In this short excerpt, we see the phrase _"I think..."_ four separate times. Anything said following, _"I think..."_ obviously expresses personal ideas (i.e., the speaker's ideology) about the subject at hand. And the criticism, _"...the president has come to approach the problems we face in very ideological, absolutist terms,"_ is also self-defeating because it is followed by the absolutist statement, _"...I think that has been a mistake."_ When leaders speak this way, they teach a hollow ethic.

Everyone relies on absolutes, but relativists try to hide that they do. Because they claim not to believe objective standards for right and wrong exist, they elevate their own standards as absolutes then prescribe them for others to follow (today's cardinal virtue, "tolerance," and Obama's "pragmatism").

---

*Pragmatism says that truth is defined by what works at the present time–a blatantly relativistic philosophy. Truth is determined by immediate, practical consequences. Under pragmatism, is it true that abortion is okay? It is if the woman determines that the consequences of ending the pregnancy don't outweigh her other interests.

This worldview is embodied in the diplomatic sounding yet prescriptive Root Idea behind Moral objections:

"People should decide for themselves what is right or wrong."

digging up the Moral ROOT IDEA

A relativist's own statements are his biggest enemy. They either apply only to himself ("That's true for you but not for me") or they are self-defeating absurdities ("There is no absolute truth!"). But the point is not just to show the skeptic that he is being self-contradictory he may not care. You want him to understand how this philosophy will affect him in the real world. If he decides for himself what he thinks is right and everyone else does the same, then he should expect chaos, not social harmony. To expose this Root Idea, *"People should decide for themselves what is right or wrong,"* ask the Probing Question,

"What is your standard for right and wrong?"

A helpful technique to couple with the Probing Question is to simply ask, "**Why?**" when a moral relativist makes any statement about what people "should" (p. 82) do.[4] The following examples show how this works in conversation:

A) *You:* "I don't see how anyone can support abortion."
   Skeptic: "I think people should respect other people's opinions."
   You: **Why?** You mean it's wrong not to do that?"
   Skeptic: "Of course it is."
   You: **"What is your standard for right and wrong?"**
   Skeptic: "Myself," "My heart,"or, "I do what I feel is right."
   You: "So, how can you impose on me what you feel is right? If you respect my opinion, shouldn't I do what I feel is right?

B)
SKEPTIC: "How could a good God send anyone to hell?"
(i.e., "A good God should not send anyone to hell.")
YOU: "Why? Is that wrong?"
SKEPTIC: "Of course it is."
YOU: **"What is your standard for right and wrong?"**
SKEPTIC: "Myself," "My heart,"or, "I do what I feel is right."
YOU: "So, you think God should do what you feel is right?
What if other people feel differently? Whom should God follow?"

In exchange (A), the skeptic attempts to be morally neutral by saying that all opinions should be equally respected*, yet he goes on to say that it's wrong if they are not. In exchange (B), the skeptic objects to God's standard, but then he plays God by using his own standard to judge God. In both cases, you are making him aware that he is not neutral and that he expects everyone else to comply with his standards.

MORAL illustrations

A powerful way to illustrate the self-defeating nature of relativism is to apply the statement to itself.[5] Several examples of this technique are shown in the *Group 1: Petards* section of Moral Red-Flag Words in the next chapter (p. 70).

---

*All *people* should be equally respected and should have equal opportunity to present ideas, but not all *ideas* are equally true. Relativists don't believe that they are either. See *exclusive*, p. 73 and *diversity*, p. 78.

HOISTED BY ONE'S OWN PETARD

"There is a gray zone between black and white and that's where most of the truth lives."[1]

- Rosie O'Donnell

8: MORAL RED-FLAG WORDS

A relativist's argument stands or falls on his ability to reshape words, so our ability to clarify words is the key to defusing relativism. There is no need to cite outside evidence or create illustrations to expose the holes in a moral skeptic's objection; his own statements are the illustrations. For this reason, the list of Red-Flag Words in the Moral category is larger than in the other three categories. These are familiar words, but they are distorted and redefined so often that we need renewed awareness of them in conversations.

CAUTION: don't zing

Because exposing the flaws of moral objections relies a great deal on turning the skeptic's words against him, be careful not to be confrontational. The point is not to zing the skeptic with a snappy comeback. If we are really serious about sharing truth, we have to respect the individual. Responding with something like, *"What I hear you saying is..."* in the right tone helps to head off a confrontational exchange.

know the definition of truth

The first word in the moral category we need to define before we go to the alphabetical list of Red-Flag Words is *truth*. Understanding truth sets the stage for understanding moral skepticism in general. The other Red-Flag Words will be divided into three groups: *Petards, Labels,* and *Impostors.*

"TRUTH"

SKEPTIC'S MEANING

Whatever is true for me (subjective truth)

SUBJECTIVE TRUTH

Moral skeptics attempt to use internal (subjective) preferences as the standard for deciding truth about things in the external world, especially moral decisions. An example of an internal standard for truth is, *"Snickers is the best tasting candy bar."* This may be subjectively true because it says something about the speaker's taste. However, it says nothing objectively true about the candy bar such as its ingredients, shape, or color that can be confirmed by outside evidence.[2] The statement, *"Snickers is the best tasting candy bar,"* is "true for you but not for me." Beliefs can contradict each other, but truths cannot. "True for you but not for me" doesn't work when a doctor tells us we have a disease, when the bank tells us we're overdrawn, or when a police officer tells us we were speeding.[3] The reality of these situations overrides our feelings about them. We need reality (outside evidence) to shed light on moral decisions.

OBJECTIVE TRUTH

"The Empire State Building is in New York" is a statement of objective truth. It is true whether or not I believe it regardless of my feelings about the building or the city. Moral ideas are objectively true. They are proven true when external reality backs them up no matter what our opinion of them is. Whatever is *real* (*reality,* p. 81-82) is also *true*.

Group 1: *Petards*

A petard was a medieval bomb. To be "hoisted by one's own petard" is to be blown up by one's own bomb. People utter petards when they use words that destroy their own arguments (self-defeating statements). Here are a few humorous examples:

- *"I plan to be more spontaneous."* >> "Plan" is a petard for anyone trying to be spontaneous.
- *"Words don't matter."* >> Words are petards for anyone who must use words to say that they don't matter.

Or try these:

- *"I'd give my right arm to be ambidextrous."*
- *"All extremists should be shot."*[4]
- *"Nostalgia isn't what it used to be."*

Moral relativists create petards by stating absolutes or by making value judgments because absolutes and value judgments defy their worldview. Since they claim that moral absolutes don't exist (truth is a "gray zone") but use absolute terms such as the following list, their arguments are self-defeating:

- "EACH/EVERY(ONE)"
- "ALL/NONE (NO ONE)"
- "BLACK/WHITE"
- "RIGHT/WRONG"
- "GOOD/EVIL"
- "BETTER/BEST/WORST"
- "FAIR/UNFAIR"

The way to respond to petards is simply to *apply the speaker's statement to itself*, thereby letting the argument blow itself up. Look at these examples:

- *"**All** truth is relative."* ☙ Is that statement a relative truth?
- *"There is a **gray** zone between **black** and **white** and that's where most of the truth lives."* ☙ Is that statement *gray* (sort of true), or *black* and *white* (absolutely true)?
- "**Everyone** should believe in relative truth." ☙ Is that statement a relative truth?
- "**No one** *has the whole truth."* ☙ Is that statement the whole truth?
- *"Truth should be decided by **each** individual."* ☙ Are you deciding that truth for me?
- "**All** truth depends on your perspective." ☙ Is that just your perspective?
- "**All** truth is subjective." ☙ Is that statement a subjective truth?
- *"That's true **for you** but not **for me**."* ☙ Is that statement only true for you or for everybody?[5]
- "Was it right or wrong to use military force to defeat the Nazis?" *I don't know...right and wrong isn't **black** or **white**."* ☙ Is that a black-and-white statement? Is it *right?*

But ending the conversation here only creates contempt. Explain that you are not trying to be a wise guy, but instead that you are trying to show how everyone uses absolutes; that's just the way truth works.

Group 2: *Labels*

This group could also be called "Stigmatizers and Discussion-enders" because these words are used by some skeptics to negatively label opponents so that they drop their argument for fear of being made to look bad. Ravi Zacharias has said, *"A stigma beats a good dogma any day."*[6] (The stigma is the label; the dogma is your argument.) Don't let a skeptic put you in a box with a label that misrepresents your view. A skeptic usually reaches for the following words when it is easier to stigmatize you rather than defend his own position:

- "CENSORSHIP"
- "DOGMA"
- "EXCLUSIVE"
- "FUNDAMENTALIST"
- "HATE"
- "INTOLERANT"
- "JUDGING"

"CENSORSHIP"

<u>SKEPTIC'S MEANING</u>

Restricting one's total freedom of personal expression

Freedom of speech and an open forum for the exchange of ideas is a good thing, but that doesn't mean the ideas are exempt from criticism. Censorship often becomes an issue in discussions involving art or communications some consider to be art. Can any form of communication inoculate itself against criticism by donning the label "art"? Merely asking people to consider the consequences of their speech and holding them accountable for their ideas is not the same as censorship. The irony is that the defensive cry of "censorship!" can effectively censor the other side by framing it as closed-minded.

"DOGMA"

SKEPTIC'S MEANING

Unbending, narrow thoughts about the world that "fundamentalists" believe because their sacred book says so

Today "dogma" is equated to certainty; to be certain about one's beliefs is to be dogmatic. Skeptics often complain that Christians *"force their beliefs down other people's throats,"* but sometimes even when a gentle manner is used to deliver truth, it can be hard to swallow. Non-compromise is not limited to Christians. Anyone willing to stand up for his argument can be labeled "dogmatic," including relativists.

"EXCLUSIVE"

SKEPTIC'S MEANING

Too narrow to see that all views are equal

Christianity is stigmatized for being exclusive, but it is no more exclusive than any other major belief system. Buddhists, Hindus, Muslims, and even moral relativists choose their worldview and *exclude* the others because they *judge* (p. 77) it to be better and believe it is *the* way. Buddhists and Hindus may say, *"We're all just taking different paths to the same place"* but they really believe that everyone will eventually wind up on the path to enlightenment not salvation, heaven, hell, or any other destination espoused by other religions.*

*Some people will take longer than others due to their particular place in this life, but ultimately they must all reincarnate until they reach Nirvana (Buddhism) or Brahman (Hinduism).

"FUNDAMENTALIST"

<u>SKEPTIC'S MEANING</u>

Someone who gives easy answers to difficult questions; someone who is certain about their beliefs

Today, "fundamentalist" denotes someone who is too closed-minded to consider other views. To be certain about one's view is to be uneducated and dangerous. It is intellectually superior to reserve judgment and to remain "open-minded" (p. 81) and ambivalent. (Never mind that one must be *certain* in order to *judge* that it is *better* to reserve judgment and remain open-minded.)

Skeptics use the "fundamentalist" label to invoke a radical picture. Consider comments by *New York Times* columnist Anthony Lewis in a 2001 interview following the printing of his final op-ed column. When asked if he had drawn any "big conclusion" after 50 years of news commentary, Lewis stated:

> One [conclusion] is that certainty is the enemy of decency and humanity in people who are sure they are right, like Osama bin Laden and John Ashcroft.[7]

Although he doesn't explicitly use the term "fundamentalist," his meaning is clear: *"people who are sure they are right"* are fundamentalists. He equates two very different types of men–one an international terrorist and Islamic fundamentalist, the other a former U.S. attorney general and conservative (fundamentalist) Christian–according to the *certainty* with which they hold their beliefs, not according to the substance of those beliefs.

Lewis's comment is itself an easy answer for a difficult question, a *fundamentalist* judgment according to the skeptic's definition of the word. It begs the question, is he *certain* about his own statement? Is he *sure* that he is right? If so, according to his own criteria, he too is an *"enemy of decency and humanity."*

"HATE"

<u>SKEPTIC'S MEANING</u>

Speaking against a person's "right" (*freedom,* p. 78,80) to do what they want to do

Mere disagreement does not rise to the level of hate. As with "intolerance" (see below), the skeptic who declares that you are preaching "hate" or spewing "hate speech" mischaracterizes your opposition to an *idea* as being opposition to the *person* expressing the idea. Disagreeing with some ideas, lifestyles, and choices to protect an individual or society expresses something closer to *love* (p. 80) than hate.

"INTOLERANT"

<u>SKEPTIC'S MEANING</u>

Disagreeing with my point of view

"Tolerance" has become *the* cardinal law in popular culture. When moral skeptics label someone who disagrees with them with the scarlet "I" of "intolerance," they miss the fact that *disagreement* is the foundation of true tolerance.[8] If I already *agree* with someone, then I don't need to tolerate their view. If both sides are honest, disagreement can bring truth into sharper focus.

I am expressing true tolerance when I *disagree* with a point of view, yet respect the person's right to express it. Today, however, *disagreement itself is considered intolerance*–a tactic used to shut down the dialogue, stigmatize the opponent, and allow the person declaring "intolerance" to have the last word. At which point we could ask, "Why are you being intolerant of my alleged intolerance?" The misuse of "intolerant" is a way to pressure wholesale acceptance of a view without regard to its validity. Christians should welcome the expression of opposing views as long as a forum exists that allows critical examination of those views.

Today, however, *disagreement itself is considered intolerance*—a tactic used to shut down the dialogue, stigmatize the opponent, and allow the person declaring "intolerance" to have the last word.

"JUDGING"

Being judgmental; unable to accept an idea or person who is different from the one judging

"Judge not" is perhaps the most habitually quoted commandment from Scripture that skeptics throw back at believers. However, Jesus is very clear about what He means in Matthew 7:1-5. Skeptics who cite this passage fail to include verse 5: *"You hypocrite, first take the plank out of your own eye, and then you will see clearly to remove the speck from your brother's eye."* Jesus warns against being hypocritical, condemning others for sins you still practice. He does not prohibit making a right judgment. In fact, He explicitly affirms it in John 7:24: *"Stop judging by mere appearances, and make a right judgment."*

The moral relativist's charge that others are "judging" him for merely opposing his ideas is itself *a judgment*. Everyone makes judgments, including relativists, otherwise they couldn't determine that relativism is better than other views. The real issue is whether a person is being *judgmental*, making a decision without considering the evidence.

Group 3: *Impostors*

Skeptics sometimes try to smuggle self-serving ideas into a discussion by disguising them in universally accepted, edifying language. These imposter terms allow the real ideas behind them to slip by without scrutiny or make those who do scrutinize them look mean-spirited. After all, only "mean-spirited" people could possibly oppose "diversity," "freedom," and "love." Here is a short list of *Impostors:*

- "DIVERSITY"
- "FREEDOM"
- "LOVE"
- "PROGRESSIVE" ("OPEN-MINDED")
- "REALITY"
- "SHOULD"

"DIVERSITY"

<u>SKEPTIC'S MEANING</u>

All cultures and groups as well as their ideas should be equally respected

CELEBRATE DIVERSITY! has become a popular mantra. True diversity makes the world interesting and challenges us to look at things from another point of view. True diversity allows evaluation of and disagreement about differing viewpoints. However, like its twin brother, "tolerance," today's "diversity" uses a group's racial, ethnic, religious, or sexual identity to shield that group's ideas from critique; *diverse people are equal, therefore, their ideas should be equal.* Opposition to the *ideas* is framed as prejudice against the *people* representing those ideas. The ideas then get a free pass regardless of their validity and are foisted on society as feel-good experiments. What if the FDA approved drugs using this philosophy?

Nearly any behavior can be defended under the guise of "diversity." According to our relativistic culture, those who don't buy into the imposter definition of diversity are "prejudiced," "bigoted," "closed-minded," "intolerant," and "exclusive." But relativists don't respect all opinions equally either; they believe "diversity" is better than other views. Should all people be equally respected due to their God-given value? Absolutely. But even sincere, kind, interesting individuals of diverse stripes can promote ideas that history and evidence prove faulty.

"FREEDOM"

"Freedom consists not in doing what we like,
but in having the right to do what we ought."
-Pope John Paul II[9]

<u>SKEPTIC'S MEANING</u>

People should be able to do as they please (as long as they don't hurt anyone else)

Like its twin brother, "tolerance," today's "diversity" uses a group's racial, ethnic, religious, or sexual identity to shield that group's ideas from critique; *diverse people are equal, therefore, their ideas should be equal.*

The dictionary lists a synonym for "freedom" that is seldom heard today, *liberty.* Liberty carries the idea of freedom with limits or with responsibility. Of course no one is allowed to do as he pleases. Laws create greater freedom precisely because they restrict some behaviors. Relativists often ask, *"How does it hurt you if someone wants to engage in behavior X?"* And the qualifier, *"...as long as it's done in the privacy of their own home"* is usually added. This response suggests that as long as someone's behavior is not in direct contact with you or is done in private, then it is harmless. But try that reasoning with these examples: *"How does it hurt you if I beat my wife?";* *"How does it hurt you if abuse my pet?"; "How does it hurt you if I'm a racist?"*

Obviously direct contact is not the only means of doing harm. We all pay a price for STDs, high illegitimacy rate, pornography addiction, drugs, abuse, and racism even if we are not directly involved. Privacy does not magically erase the consequences of irresponsible freedom. But Romans 6:22 describes the biblical idea of freedom: *"But now that you have been set free from sin and have become slaves to God, the benefit you reap leads to holiness, and the result is eternal life."*

"LOVE"

SKEPTIC'S MEANING

Affection toward another that makes both parties feel good

The highest love, *agape*, is not based on feelings. It desires the greatest good for another person regardless of how it makes them or the person expressing it feel. Relationships that only feed the feelings of the parties involved through physical or emotional gratification, yet ignore the ultimate well-being of the persons, are not based on true love. If a child wants to drink glass cleaner because it looks pretty, you stop him because your love for him values his well-being above his feelings. Tough love is unpopular because it initiates growth, which can be uncomfortable. Ephesians 4:14-15 describes tough love this way: *"Then we will no longer be infants.... Instead, speaking the truth in love, we will in all things grow up into him who is the Head, that is, Christ."*

"PROGRESSIVE (OPEN-MINDED)"

"Merely having an open mind is nothing.
The object of opening the mind, as of opening the mouth,
is to shut it again on something solid."

- G. K. Chesterton[10]

SKEPTIC'S MEANING

Newer ideas are better (as long as they aren't "exclusive")

Relativists fear ideas they believe will threaten their freedom of personal expression. They believe truly enlightened individuals should be open-minded enough to "live and let live." What they ignore is that ideas have consequences. According to the definition of "progressive," ideas that cause society to go backward should be discarded. Yet many relativists support choices that when taken to their logical conclusions result in a deteriorating society, not a progressing one. Examples include: public policies that deconstruct the institution of marriage; procedures that abort future persons; and an unwillingness to describe any form of expression as "obscene."

"REALITY"

SKEPTIC'S MEANING

Whatever my preferences tell me is true

In a conversation when a relativist begins to realize the contradictory nature of his worldview, he may seek refuge by pretending not to know what "reality" is. The most obvious moral questions suddenly become difficult issues for him. But he can avoid the issue of right and wrong altogether if he can toy with you by saying that the world is an illusion. If a skeptic says something like, *"How do we know what reality is?,"* a quick way to bring the conversation back into focus is to ask him, *"Who is asking the question?"*[11] He must either confess that *he* is–admitting that he is *real*–or continue the charade that you are speaking to an illusion. If he persists, you could ask him to test his theory by standing in traffic or by giving you his wallet.

"SHOULD"

SKEPTIC'S MEANING
Conforming to my idea of right and wrong

> "So for me personally, talking about absolute truth
> is a nonsensical way to talk, and Christian theologians
> shouldn't talk in that way."
>
> -Tony Jones, National Coordinator of *Emergent*[12]

In trying to appeal to the postmodern culture, the Emergent Church movement is actually a peddler of postmodern, self-defeating philosophy. Tony Jones begins his comment with *"...for me personally"* but then ends it with a prescription for what others *"shouldn't"* do. This exposes his dependence on absolute truth in the midst of his denial that it exists. It shows that his standard is fixed (absolute) and not only applies to himself but to others. Is he *absolutely* sure that *"talking about absolute truth is a nonsensical way to talk"*? If so, then he is talking nonsense.

"Should" may appear to be an insignificant word, but it is pivotal in understanding moral relativism.[13] A moral skeptic's personal goal is to escape the word "should" (or "ought") so that he can avoid moral absolutes and behave any way he chooses. However, he cannot express his own opinions about moral questions and at the same time avoid "should." What he really believes is that "should" *should* apply to everyone except himself. He says he believes individuals are their own standard of morality–no one *should* tell others what they *should* do–but therein lies the contradiction. In effect he is saying, *"The*

A moral skeptic's personal goal is to escape the word "should" (or "ought") so that he can avoid moral absolutes and behave any way he chooses.

right thing to do is to let people decide what is the right thing to do." But his own idea of right is the standard for deciding this.

Everyone has a standard for right and wrong; no one is neutral. The moment a relativist uses "should," he reveals that he is really an absolutist with a standard he expects others to follow. If the moral skeptic wants to be consistent, when faced with a moral question he must: 1) remain silent about what he thinks others *should* do,[14] 2) follow up every moral judgment with *"...but that's just my opinion,"* or 3) say, *"Whatever."*

Again, the best way to respond to any moral objection that uses "should" is to ask, **"WHY?"** and follow up with the probing question, *"What is your standard for right and wrong?"* By doing so, we can expose the fact that the skeptic's standard for right and wrong is himself which *should* have no bearing on anyone else. Here's an example:

> *Skeptic:* "Women *should* have the right to choose abortion."
> *Believer:* "**Why?** (You mean it's wrong if they don't?) What is your moral standard for that idea?"

SCIENTIFIC SKEPTICISM

SCIENTIFIC SKEPTICISM IN A NUTSHELL

The worldview behind most scientific skepticism is *naturalism* (nature is all that there is). Naturalism has serious problems as a worldview regarding the two main scientific arguments that you will most commonly encounter: the *Big Bang* (origin of the universe) argument, and the *evolution* (development of life) argument. It is important to point out to the skeptic that his naturalistic view invokes supernatural power as much as yours does. The big difference is that naturalism puts faith in the *absurd*–nature doing *super*natural things– while a theistic worldview merely puts faith in the *unseen*–a cause beyond nature that has left evidence in nature of its presence.

Don't be misled that because something is unseen it is irrational. In the case of the origin and development of our world, the unseen cause–an Intelligent Designer–is a far more rational explanation than believing that nature is able to do what science already proves that it cannot.

Evolutionists desperately need to include an Intelligence in their theory in order for it to work, but they reject one. Instead, they put faith in natural selection and mutation to produce the new information (new DNA) needed for creatures to evolve. But as we will discuss, natural selection and mutation *create nothing new*–they only remove or rearrange what is already there. But rearranging Mr. Potato Head doesn't make him G.I. Joe.

Naturalistic skeptics complain that belief in a Creator is too convenient; it is a crutch. But this smoke screen hides the convenience of their own beliefs. If there is no Creator to whom man is accountable, then he is free to do as he pleases. The downside is that man is merely the result of random processes. He has no inherent worth and no higher authority to whom he can appeal for justice. As with relativism, *might* determines *right*, and man's worth is determined by his usefulness to those in power, making him not so free after all.

"One has only to contemplate the magnitude of this task to concede that the spontaneous generation of a living organism is impossible. Yet here we are—as a result, I believe, of spontaneous generation."

- Harvard biochemist, Nobel Laureate, and evolutionist, George Wald[1]

"Imaginations run riot in conjuring up an image of our most ancient ancestor—the creature that gave rise to both apes and humans. This ancestor is not apparent in ape or human anatomy nor in the fossil record."

"Anatomy and the fossil record cannot be relied upon for evolutionary lineages. Yet palaeontologists persist in doing just this."

- Anthropologists and evolutionists, J. Lowenstein and Adrienne Zihlman, Ph.D[2]

9: THE SCIENTIFIC ROOT IDEA

SCIENTIFIC objections involve:
• Divorcing reason from faith
• The universe (Big Bang, etc.)
• Evolution

sample objections:

"God is an irrational crutch people use to explain things they don't understand."

"The Big Bang started the universe." ("Creation in six days is a nice story for kids.")

"There are so many similarities between humans and apes...it's easy to see that we evolved."

Naturalism is two-faced; it dismisses a creator's supernatural involvement in our world but credits nature with the ability to do supernatural things (or to do the "impossible" as George Wald puts it). Naturalistic skeptics will vehemently deny that faith plays into their worldview, but let's test their beliefs according to scientific requirements.

A belief has a scientific basis if it has been *observed* and *repeated,* * although an eyewitness is not necessary to make a scientific determination. For past events that cannot be directly observed, scientists can legitimately base conclusions on similar repeatable events in the present. So we need to find out if any repeatable events in the present support the following beliefs that naturalistic scientists say *happened only once* in the past:[3]

A) *The leap from nothing to everything (before the Big Bang)*

The Big Bang only asserts that things in the universe were once together because we can observe that they are now moving apart. It can not explain how they came into being from nothing. Something coming from nothing within a natural system is blatantly irrational.

---

*Observation and repetition are the two basic components of scientific inquiry.

B) *The leap from non-life to life*

Life erupting from non-life has been soundly disproven by Pasteur, Urey and Miller (who under rigged conditions produced a noxious mixture of right- and left-handed amino acids that disrupt formation of biological proteins), and others.[4] But suppose they were all wrong. Spontaneous generation is still a non-scientific belief because it rests on a one-time, unsubstantiated event.

C) *The leaps from one species to another (fish to reptiles, reptiles to birds, apes to humans, etc.)*

As for the origin of species, evolutionists claim that we do have evidence that species evolved into other species. They say the small adaptations we see in creatures now are the kind that over time added up to large evolutionary changes in the past.* However, as we will discuss in the definition of "evolution" (p. 99), *speciation* (changing from one species to another) and *adaptation* (changes within a species) are two vastly different processes.

Scientists generally discard one-time occurrences (anomalies, flukes) as invalid evidence. But evolutionists retain examples A, B, and C as cornerstones of their beliefs. Because most SCIENTIFIC objections are based on faith that nature can do supernatural things, they stem from the Root Idea:

"The natural world is all that there is."

(Nature can do godlike things.)

The skeptic may counter our view with, *"What scientific basis (repeated examples) do we have that indicates an* <u>*intelligence*</u> *may have caused life?"*

The fact is they are all around us because the answer lies in *information* (p. 101). Complex, meaningful information does not arise by chance, and it cannot be reduced to physical causes. Therefore, it is not a blind leap of faith to conclude that living things containing the voluminous code of DNA demand an intelligent cause.

---

*If these changes have occurred for millions of years, there should be a massive amount of fossils and a current population of animals and humans so large that the earth couldn't hold them. Consider human population alone. The current world population growth rate is 1.7%. If we start just one million years ago with two people who reproduce at a rate of only 0.01%, the population would number 10^{43} today–many times more than the stars in the universe.[5]

Scientists generally discard one-time
occurrences (anomalies, flukes)
as invalid evidence. But evolutionists
retain significant ones as cornerstones
of their beliefs.

why naturalism?

> "So how could you ask me to believe in God when
> there's absolutely no evidence that I can see?
> I do believe...that there are scientific explanations
> for phenomena that we call mystical because
> we don't know any better."
>
> -Jodie Foster in an interview regarding her 1997 film *Contact* [6]

Jodie Foster probably doesn't realize that she has exchanged one source of faith for another. She excludes God because of a presumed lack of evidence, yet puts her faith in unseen future explanations. But does naturalistic science earn this show of faith? As we saw in the last section, it disregards fundamental scientific principles and repeatable findings in favor of one-time miraculous events.

So why do skeptics continue to embrace naturalism? I think there are three basic reasons. The first is that nature makes no moral demands. It is easier to credit it as the source for everything than to make one's self accountable to a relational, transcendent God.

The second reason is fear of the stigma of creationism. The simple Genesis creation account is portrayed as a childish, embarrassing alternative in a culture that accepts evolution as fact. Christians and non-Christians alike attempt to reconcile Genesis and evolution because they don't want to be considered Bible-thumpers or ignoramuses. Consequently, they settle for God-guided (theistic) evolution. But is God-guided evolution a viable option? (See *BONUS POINT V*, [p. 131] for why it is not.)

The third reason people choose naturalism stems from intellectualism. For intellectual skeptics, creationism and Intelligent Design seem like a cop-out. They appear to be intellectually vapid and simplistic ("God did it"). In actuality, however, these approaches are unafraid to allow the possibility that non-natural causes can make better sense of the data. For example, I.D. is already used in forensics, archaeology, cryptography, and SETI (Search for Extraterrestrial Intelligence) to determine if events are random chance, natural law, or caused by intelligence. [7]

digging up the Scientific ROOT IDEA

"If you ask people why they are convinced of the truth
of their religion, they don't appeal to heredity.
Put like that it sounds too obviously stupid.
Nor do they appeal to evidence. There isn't any,
and nowadays the better educated admit it.
No, they appeal to faith. Faith is the great cop-out,
the great excuse to evade the need to think and
evaluate evidence. Faith is belief in spite of,
even perhaps because of, the lack of evidence.
The worst thing is that the rest of us are supposed to
respect it: to treat it with kid gloves."

- Richard Dawkins, celebrated evolutionist, vehement atheist[8]

"Faith is not the enemy of science–*true* science."
- Dr. Zaius, Minister of Ape Science/Chief Defender of the Faith,
The Planet of the Apes (1968)[9]

The classic film adapted from Pierre Boulle's novel, *The Planet of the Apes,* is full of irony that has fresh meaning in light of the recent debates over evolution. In the film, the orangutan scientists led by Dr. Zaius also serve as philosophers and religious zealots who hide evidence that intelligent humans once ruled the world. Some scientists today hold a similar bias.

Today's naturalistic scientists would like us to believe that their conclusions are "pure science" cleansed of any philosophical bias. But the irony is that while informed believers want to discuss the evidence for and against evolution, evolutionists like Dawkins guard their philosophy with religious fervor in spite of the evidence. (Ben Stein's film *Expelled: No Intelligence Allowed* [2008] is an astute exposé of this practice.)

Zaius is convinced that humans must be exterminated because they threaten ape civilization. Similarly, Dawkins believes anti-evolutionist thinking (and any religious belief) is a sickness that should be eradicated (*The God Delusion*). But unlike Zaius, Dawkins is unwilling to admit that even science and scientists rely to some extent on faith.

Evolution is scientifically broken (see *mutation* and *natural selection,* pp. 107-111) and evidentially bankrupt. The problem is that it has the bully pulpit; anything that contradicts it is ridiculed as non-science, religion, or idiocy. Evolution's legitimacy is not open to debate–it is absolute doctrine. An army of sources that feed the skeptic's mind and imagination will probably squash your direct attempts to disprove the theory. Public education, college professors, experts like Dawkins, major news and scientific magazines, well-produced, well-funded educational TV programming, and Hollywood films capture the imagination of the public in favor of evolution. In these mediums, a non-evolutionary perspective is as hard to find as are the missing links in the fossil record. Your work is cut out for you if you try to discredit these sources or to debate every example the skeptic brings up.

correct the argument

Before we engage specific questions, we need to correct the argument. We should reject the assumption that evolution is "science" and non-evolution is "religion." We need to point out that *faith* is as central to the scientific skeptic's worldview as it is to ours. The real argument is not *faith* versus *science* but rather, *informed faith* versus *blind faith. Everyone* relies on faith, physicist and preacher alike; the hypocrisy is pretending that you don't.

"How much faith is required for that belief?"

We are asserting that his presumed scientific beliefs involve as much or more faith than evidence. This conversation can take two main routes:

1) A **Big-Bang** (origin of the universe) discussion
   or,
2) An **evolution** (development of life) discussion.

Following is a sample Big-Bang discussion. You can respond in an evolution discussion by clarifying the true meanings of the evolution Red-Flag Words in the next chapter.

> *SKEPTIC:* "The Big Bang started the universe." (p. 97)
> *YOU:* **"How much faith is required for that belief?"**
> *SKEPTIC:* "What faith? I'm talking about science."
> *YOU:* "Well, it takes a lot of faith to believe the universe created itself. Self-creation doesn't make sense."
> *SKEPTIC:* "Maybe the universe is eternal...maybe this is just one of many universes."
> *YOU:* "Sounds like you don't have a lot of evidence for that."
> *SKEPTIC:* "Okay, if God did it, where did God come from?"
> *YOU:* "We have two choices: believe the absurd or believe in the unseen. The absurd choice is that nature created itself. That leaves us with one option: an unseen cause outside of nature.

"The extreme rarity of transitional forms in the fossil record persists as the trade secret of paleontology."

- Stephen J. Gould, late preeminent Harvard paleontologist
  and evolutionary biologist'

10: SCIENTIFIC RED-FLAG WORDS

Although an evolution apostle to the end, Gould realized that the absence of billions of transitional fossils that should exist after aeons of evolving creatures was more than just a hiccup in evolutionary theory. But the physical evidence isn't the only thing missing–so is the logic. In this section, we will look at the basic components of evolution and uncover the monkey wrenches instead of the missing links.

The following terms are a short list, but they are the foundation for most of the scientific objections you will face. Evolutionists may try to intimidate you with obscure examples or bury you under scientific jargon, but it is their spin on the basic principles below that is vulnerable to examination.

- "BIG BANG"
- "EVOLUTION"
- "INFORMATION"
- "MUTATION"
- "NATURAL SELECTION"

"BIG BANG"

SKEPTIC'S MEANING

The sudden uncaused beginning of the universe based on the idea that objects are moving away from each other suggesting that they were once together in a single location

Big Bang theory does not completely oppose the biblical worldview. Like the Genesis creation account, it implies a beginning *ex nihilo* (out of nothing), but unlike Genesis it leaves out a Beginner. The Big Bang model has gained the most notoriety although it is not without problems.* But the details of the theory are not the real issue. The real issue is, *what started it?*

---

*The clustering of matter in the universe instead of its even distribution is a major puzzle.[2]

If the skeptic insists that *"the Big Bang started the universe,"* you could proceed with the line of reasoning we discussed at the end of the previous chapter. But the skeptic might object that you are bringing philosophy into the discussion when it is really about "science." Or if he has been keeping up with bleeding-edge scientific conjecture, he might say that you just don't understand dark matter, string theory, or multiple universes. The fact is, he doesn't either–cosmologists admit the highly speculative nature of these theories. In other words, they require some measure of faith.

shifting from the Big Bang to evolution

To move the discussion along, it's okay to concede (hypothetically) that matter and energy popped into existence out of nothing via the Big Bang and that humans evolved from non-living matter. These huge concessions may seem to put you on the evolutionist's turf, but they actually limit the discussion to the heart of the debate: *whether or not NATURAL SELECTION and MUTATION can really drive evolution, and where INFORMATION comes from if not from an Intelligence.* Rightly understanding these concepts exposes gaping holes in the theory.

Before debating how evolution supposedly works, first clarify the meaning of the word "evolution" itself, which is often a vehicle to bait and switch the concepts of the discussion.

"EVOLUTION"

<u>SKEPTIC'S MEANING</u>

Depending on the audience: *a)* "change over time"; *b)* the ability of creatures to transform into entirely different species

"The theory that all the living forms in the world have arisen from a single source which itself came from an inorganic form."

- General Theory of Evolution (GTE), Gerald A. Kerkut[3]

After reading the GTE, it is easy to see why evolutionists try to popularize their theory with students and lay audiences by claiming that evolution merely means "change over time." But that's like saying a personal computer is merely a *changed* typewriter. The GTE actually exposes the much more radical kind of change that evolutionary theory presupposes–all life spontaneously erupted from *"an inorganic form,"* i.e., a rock or goo (never mind how the rock or goo got there). But leading evolutionists can't just stand up and say, *"We believe all life evolved from a rock!"* They must massage the terms in order to make them palatable to the general public. When used by evolutionists, the word "evolution" is itself a mutating term.

Evolutionists are selling the idea that a lot of little changes in a creature, *microevolution*, eventually add up to big changes, *macroevolution*. However, the term "microevolution" is spin for *adaptation*. Microevolution, or more accurately "change within a kind," does not lead to macroevolution–*it eliminates the need for it*. If a population of creatures can *adapt* to its environment because of the genes it already has, it has no need to evolve. This makes the mechanism of evolution self-defeating. While microevolution (adaptation) is a reality, macroevolution (e.g. a reptile changing into a bird) lacks validity both in theory and in evidence. Here is an example of each:

Microevolution does not lead to macroevolution–*it eliminates the need for it.* If a population of creatures can *adapt* to its environment because of the genes it already has, it has no need to evolve.

Microevolution - Over a few generations, a mosquito population becomes resistant to insecticide.

Macroevolution - Over a few million years, a type of lizard gradually becomes a bird.

These two concepts are vastly different, not merely stages of the same process as evolutionists would have us believe. The discussion of the next three terms will illustrate the fatal flaws of macroevolution.

"INFORMATION"

SKEPTIC'S MEANING

How we describe the order we see in living things that only look designed

The concept of information creates huge problems for evolutionary theory. It refutes two key assumptions of evolution: 1) complex living things can arise at random, and 2) everything comes from matter.

randomness does not create information

We live in the information age, but what is information? Information is a combination of symbols that creates a meaningful message–a code, language, blueprint, etc. A symphony is meaningful information, but noise from a jackhammer is not. Abraham Lincoln's *Gettysburg Address* is meaningful information, but a pile of Scrabble letters is not. A Ferrari is meaningful information, but a heap of scrap metal is not. What separates meaningful information from non-meaningful information? Meaningful information must be both *complex* and *specified*.[4]

Information that is complex and specified does not happen at random. You could create complexity by dumping a pile of Scrabble letters on the floor, but produce no specified message. You might randomly produce a specified message such as "C-A-T" by dumping out letters, although C-A-T is not a complex message.[5] But your chances of dumping letters on the floor and getting "F-O-U-R-S-C-O-R-E-A-N-D-S-E-V-E-N-Y-E-A-R-S-A-G-O" is highly unlikely. And getting the complete *Gettysburg Address* (a short speech) is beyond realistic. If you saw the Scrabble version of the *Gettysburg Address* on the floor, you would conclude that it was intentional (designed).

We know it is designed because we instinctively know that words are systems of letters; sentences are systems of words; paragraphs are systems of sentences; and speeches are systems of paragraphs. Such systems cannot form without foresight, planning, and intention. In other words, a *system* –not an independent part–*is the most basic unit of any complex, meaningful structure* (see mousetrap opposite page). But evolutionists would like us to believe that complex systems such as those found in living things arose part-by-part. Consider this statement by Richard Dawkins:

> *The great beauty of Darwin's theory of evolution is that it explains how complex, difficult to understand things could have arisen step by plausible step, from simple, easy to understand beginnings. We start our explanation from almost infinitely simple beginnings: pure hydrogen and a huge amount of energy. Our scientific, Darwinian explanations carry us through a series of well-understood gradual steps to all the spectacular beauty and complexity of life.[6]*

This is a brazen exaggeration. Don't let an evolutionist off the hook who suggests that life evolved from "simple beginnings"–there is no such thing. The beginnings would have to be complex also. The most primitive, single-celled bacteria that evolutionists say began life on earth would have needed working systems including some form of digestive system and reproductive system from the very beginning. Such systems are immensely complex.

cont. p. 104

illustration: *Mousetrap*

   The concept of information and complexity can be abstract for many, but it can also be unfamiliar to people who consider themselves educated regarding evolution. To illustrate for a skeptic that the simplest structures (living or inanimate) must at minimum begin with fully functioning systems, use the mousetrap example popularized by biochemist Michael Behe in <u>Darwin's Black Box</u>.[7] A mousetrap is a simple system, yet it is irreducibly complex; no more parts can be removed and it maintain its basic function.[8] The chances of a mousetrap coming together at random are astronomical, even more so for living things that supposedly evolved. The first step of existence for the most basic living things are working systems vastly more complex than a mousetrap; anything less would mean evolution never gets off the ground.

Could the mousetrap work if just one part were missing or out of place?

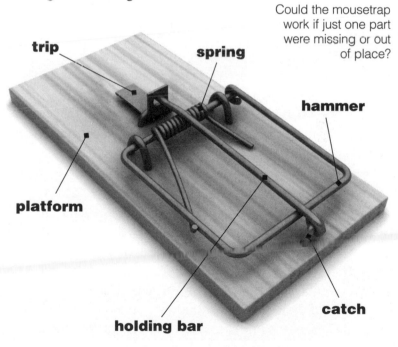

trip

spring

hammer

platform

holding bar

catch

A *system*–not independent parts–
is the most basic unit of any complex,
meaningful structure.

Natural selection (p. 109), a presumed key player in evolution, has no foresight to hold on to single parts for potential systems until all of the parts are not only available but in the right places. If they are not all available and in the right places, natural selection eliminates them as non-functioning debris. This means the process of evolution could not start until all the parts for vital systems for the earliest creature randomly and instantly appeared in all the right places–a mathematical absurdity.*

information is not *material stuff*

Evolutionists attempt to explain the world in terms of only physical/material causes. But the curious thing about information is that it is *non-physical;* it does not arise out of material stuff.[10]

Materials such as paper, discs, and DNA molecules are only carriers of information. For example, the information in the *Gettysburg Address* exists outside of the paper and ink Lincoln used to write it. It could exist just as well on an audio CD, on the Internet, or engraved in stone. Yet we cannot describe this famous speech by reducing it to paper and ink, coated plastic, pixels, or stone. It did not begin in these materials; it began in Abraham Lincoln's mind.

An evolutionist might say, *"But Lincoln's mind is merely reactions of brain chemicals."* In other words, Lincoln's mind was the result of random, material (chemical) causes. But this would mean that the *Gettysburg Address* is the result of random, material causes too because it came from Lincoln's mind. But as we have discussed, complex systems such as speeches (not to mention human brains) don't arise out of randomness; they are the product of intention and planning (design). This means that Lincoln's mind and ours are something more than just chemicals. Our minds have the power of intentionality; our brains are the medium for communicating it.

Just as the *Gettysburg Address* is the not the product

*Mathematician William Dembski has calculated the probability that a flagellum, the rotary tail that powers a bacteria (considered the simplest form of life), through liquid, could form at random to be 1 in 10^{1170}. This number is vastly larger than the estimated number of atoms in the universe (10^{80}).[9]

Information is *non-physical;*
it does not arise out of material stuff.

But whether or not a beneficial mutation can be proven is a moot point. The critical question to ask about mutations is, *"Can they generate new information (new DNA)?"*

of paper and ink, DNA, the blueprint for living things, is not the product of a random soup of chemical compounds. By all accounts, it is a code or language so complex that no material causes could have created it; *it demands an author.* Only mind, not matter, can generate meaningful information. The more complex the information, the more prodigious the mind needed to produce it.

However, evolutionists cannot accept this. They dismiss the idea of design and say that creatures just *look* designed. For them, design is only apparent, merely a description we impose on the order we see in living things. They maintain that natural selection and mutation are able to generate the DNA required to create new species. Let's take a look at these two key concepts.

"MUTATION"

SKEPTIC'S MEANING

Random genetic improvements from one generation to the next allowing an organism to move up the evolutionary ladder

Evolutionists are intent on identifying beneficial mutations. Malaria-resistant sickle cells and antibiotic-resistant bacteria are two popular examples.* But whether or not a beneficial mutation can be proven is a moot point. The critical question to ask about mutations is, *"Can they generate new information (new DNA)?"* Evolutionists bring mutations into the theory because they need a naturalistic way to introduce new DNA into an organism so that it can evolve into a *new* creature.

However, mutations only *degrade* or *rearrange* existing genetic information; they don't generate new information. Genes are like sequences of letters (code) that act as blueprints and instructions for a creature's form and functions. A genetic mutation is analogous to the following sequence of letters:

---

*Although carriers of sickle cells are more resistant to malaria, sickle cell disease is far from a genetic advantage. Sickle-cell disease creates severe health risks including organ damage, infections, and other serious problems.[11] Likewise, mutated, antibiotic-resistant bacteria do not have a true advantage because they can't reproduce as fast as non-mutated bacteria, so they die out more quickly.[12]

iwanttoevolve   < normal gene
iwånTtøevolvé < mutation (degraded)
ovatevnotlwie < mutation (rearranged)
øvåtevnoTlwié < mutation (degraded and rearranged)

No matter how you degrade or rearrange the message "iwanttoevolve," you either get "iwanttoevolve" with slight modifications or you get gibberish. No new letters arise to create a new, more complex message.

In the same way, you could never create Wikipedia using the information from a Twitter message no matter how you rearranged it–Wikipedia contains much more information. Or suppose you have the blueprints for a Mercedes Benz. Could you repeatedly photocopy them hoping that a copy one hundred generations later would randomly accumulate spots and smudges that transformed it into blueprints for the Space Shuttle or even an upgraded design for the Mercedes? The blueprint quality would get worse, not better, the more it was duplicated.

Mutations are incapable of generating new genetic information. But evolutionists hold out faith that the hero of their theory, natural selection, can make it all work out.

"NATURAL SELECTION"

<u>SKEPTIC'S MEANING</u>

The mechanism by which increasingly organized and complex organisms come into being; creatures with adaptable traits survive to pass on their genes, while less adaptable creatures die out of a group

Natural selection is the blind watchmaker, blind because
it does not see ahead, does not plan consequences,
has no purpose in view.[13]
Cumulative selection, by slow and gradual degrees,
is the explanation, the only workable explanation that has ever
been proposed, for the existence of life's complex design.
- Richard Dawkins, *The Blind Watchmaker*[14]

Natural selection actually occurs, but it has nothing to do with accumulating complexity or with changing one species into another as Dawkins insists. Remember, "natural selection" is merely a description of a process, not a thinking, planning agent as Dawkins's blind-watchmaker analogy confirms. The important thing to note about natural selection is that it is a process of *subtraction,* not addition.[15] It *streamlines* creatures for better survival in their existing environment by removing traits less suited for that environment. It does not cross-train creatures for new environments. It cannot collect, assemble, or create new genetic features (new DNA) required to transform one kind of creature into a different kind that can survive in a completely different environment.

A mosquito population can survive the threat of insecticide because of what it *loses*, not what it gains. Mosquitoes with a genetic weakness toward a particular insecticide die off. But the surviving, resistant mosquitoes become the new core population for a "stronger" next generation. (They may be stronger only against the original insecticide but vulnerable in other ways.) Is this new resistant

The important thing to note about natural selection is that it is a process of *subtraction*, not addition.

group a sign that the mosquitoes are breaking the bonds of mosquitohood and evolving into a new creature? *No.* Their mosquito DNA dictates that they will *remain* mosquitoes. This new group has been "selected" to survive because it has *lost* the weak trait by losing the weak members of the group that carried it, not by evolving a new trait. The insecticide merely exposes a genetic resistance that these mosquitoes had all along.

Dog breeding works the same way. Today, dogs such as Pugs and Yorkies are primarily bred as lap dogs. Breeders streamline a dog population for lap sitting by selectively breeding dogs without large features. This streamlining effect is the same no matter if the selection process is intentional or natural. In a natural setting, if a variety of dogs were set loose to fend for themselves in the wild, after a few generations, the dog population would probably resemble dingoes or wild dogs more than Yorkies (i.e., bigger, stronger, faster, aggressive traits would be naturally suited for this rugged environment). But if the environment is lap sitting, dingoes don't stand a chance. The fact is that dogs *remain* dogs no matter how streamlined they become for their environment.

BIBLICAL SKEPTICISM

BIBLICAL SKEPTICISM IN A NUTSHELL

The Bible is difficult to defend in a brief exchange because it is a complex book whose image in the nonbelieving world has been shaped much more by hearsay than by firsthand inspection. Many believe that it is not inspired by God (see *inspired,* p. 26) but originated with man. How motivated would you be to read a book if the typical labels that described it were "outdated," "error-filled," and "legend"? These descriptions reflect a strident secularism in our society. Secularism is the belief that there is nothing eternal or sacred, therefore, man's ideas are governed by the here and now.[1]

The popular culture's skepticism of the Bible is reinforced by a stable of nonbelieving experts cited by the media. But how many experts *who claim Christ as their Savior* are consulted by the media to explain the Bible?* Very few. That is why we need to revive the Bible's relevance and make it compelling again.

We should acknowledge that the Bible makes amazing claims but that this is to be expected from any book that professes to be the Word of God. The question is, what evidence is consistent with this claim? We should make it clear to the skeptic that we don't believe just because "the Bible says so," but because its authenticity is consistent with history and its accurate, extensive, and vivid depiction of the human condition.

Finally, we can encourage the skeptic to not only take our word, but to read the Bible for himself (we should suggest places to start). Admit that it's okay to be skeptical of the Bible, but emphasize that one should read it with the same trust and scrutiny as one reads any other book.

---

*There are more than enough believing, intellectual giants in this field to consult. (See p. 133 for just a few.)

"How does it help us to say that the Bible is the inerrant word of God if in fact we don't have the words that God inerrantly inspired, but only the words copied by the scribes–sometimes correctly and sometimes (many times!) incorrectly?"

- Bart Ehrman, "happy agnostic," Chair of the Dept. of Religious Studies, UNC[2]

11: THE BIBLICAL ROOT IDEA

BIBLICAL objections involve:
• The Bible's relevance
• The Bible's reliability
• The Bible's authority

sample objections:

"The Bible authors were just men with their own biases."

"We can't trust the Bible because it has been corrupted by many years of copying and translation."

"The Bible no longer applies to our modern world."

the Bible's image under fire

Biblical scholar and former professing believer Bart Ehrman has gone to great lengths to convince others that the Bible is unreliable. His academic investigation of perceived fatal flaws in Bible manuscripts is his apparent reason for writing books that question the authenticity of the Bible. However, he admits that biblical investigation was not the reason his personal belief faded. While teaching at Rutgers in the 1980s on the problem of human suffering, he was impacted by the coverage of the African famine at that time. He says, *"I just began to lose it...I just couldn't believe there was a God in charge of this mess..."* Because he no longer believed God cared, his view of the Bible took a predictable turn. He says he could no longer accept *"This whole business of 'the Bible is your life, and anyone who doesn't believe it is going to roast in hell.'"*[3]

This illustrates one of the most common reasons people reject the Bible: God doesn't fit their idea of Him. Ehrman's discontent with God colors the presumed objective academic lens that informs his position. As mentioned at the beginning of this book, personal issues play a major role in unbelief.

But in addition to the Bible's marred image resulting from a person's internal struggles, the Bible must also compete against the secular culture. Beside the fact that it tells people to change things they don't want to change, its historical setting and its length make it daunting for many. Stack up God's written Word against the constant electronic feed from our culture's holy trinity–*smart phone/tablet/Internet*–and the Bible never gets off the shelf (if it were ever there). Christians today are guilty of not reading it either.* Instant, feel-good consumerism has infected the church as well.

The Bible's credibility also comes under fire because of its audacity: it records supernatural events and claims to be the Word of God. Secularists make the Bible a caricature by acknowledging some of its practical wisdom while dismissing its incredible claims. But the Bible is either entirely the Word of God or it is not. If its extraordinary content is dismissed, the remaining collection of wisdom is meaningless because it is entwined with and dependent upon the extraordinary content.

Just as Jesus cannot be accepted as merely a "good man" (he is either liar, lunatic, or Lord–or myth or guru some argue)** the Bible cannot be accepted as merely a "good book" –it is either lies, absurdities, or the Word of God. Consequently, a skeptic's view of the Bible is vague and confused because he usually relies on hearsay rather than an honest firsthand reading. He decides it must be the result of corrupted human authorship and is no more authoritative than any other book on the shelf. Therefore, we can summarize this Root Idea as:

"The Bible is man-made."
(It originated with man rather than God.)

If it is man-made, people who harbor personal animosity toward it, people who can't believe its audacious claims, and people preoccupied with the buzz of the culture don't have to worry about its influence over their lives. They can pick and choose what to accept as if it were any other book.

*The 2008 *Pew Forum on Religion and Public Life* found that 57 percent of American evangelical church attendees and 70 percent of people claiming a religious affiliation believe many roads lead to eternal life.⁴

**C.S. Lewis popularized the "trilemma." See p. 125 for *myth* argument flaws. Jesus never claimed enlightenment (p. 50) or to be a guru, but rather "the light of the world."⁵

Stack up God's written Word against the constant electronic feed from our culture's holy trinity–*smart phone/tablet/Internet*– and the Bible never gets off the shelf (if it were ever there).

digging up the Biblical ROOT IDEA

We can begin wiping off the Bible's smudged image by first questioning a skeptic's common preconceptions rather than by quoting Bible passages. In responding to arguments against the Bible's reliability, the classic approach has been to recite manuscript (bibliographic) evidence, internal evidence, and external evidence to show that the Bible is unique among historical documents (*BONUS POINT VI*, p.122). This kind of evidence is powerful, and it is advantageous for Christians to know some of it. However, a good deal of time and explanation is required to unpack it for people (nearly everyone) who are unfamiliar with the process of evaluating ancient documents. Here is an example:

> *Skeptic:* "The Bible is unreliable."
> *Christian:* "Did you know that there are more manuscripts of the New Testament dated closer to the actual events than there are for Homer's *Iliad* or Caesar's *Gallic Wars*?"
> *Skeptic:* "Ugh...I guess I'll take your word for it." *or,*
> "That's just what your sources say."

Because most people have not studied textual criticism, the value of this answer will be lost. If the skeptic himself had compared the Bible to another ancient document, then an answer like this would be appropriate. So instead of opening with this kind of material, use it as supporting information for later in the discussion.

As with the other categories, we should first engage the Root Idea that is the basis for their skepticism (*"The Bible is man-made"*). We need to present the Bible in a way they can relate to it first on a practical level, then on a transcendent level. We might start by saying something like, *"I understand your skepticism. No one ever said the Bible was an easy book."* Then we should ask the Probing Question:

"If God really gave us a book, how would we know it came from Him?"

The skeptic may try to answer or he may argue that there is no way to recognize a book from God. If he turns the question back to us, we have the opportunity to explain why we trust the Bible. That is why we need to give a better answer than, *"I just have faith."*

illustrations

The following illustrations might help you explain why the Bible is reliable and why it is more than a man-made book:

#1. Recipe

Most skeptics don't understand how the Bible was preserved or passed down. They usually assume people over the centuries played the "telephone game" by which the story was passed from person to person until the content was changed so much by the end that it is unreliable. But the telephone game has nothing to do with the Bible. Following is my version of an illustration by Christian apologist Greg Koukl that quickly explains how the Bible was preserved virtually unchanged:

A Recipe for Reliability

Suppose Grandma wants to preserve the recipe for her famous blackberry sauce. She carefully makes five hand-written copies of the original recipe card (she doesn't have email) which she gives to her five quilting buddies. They in turn make hand-written copies for each of their daughters (ten copies in all).

One day, Grandpa sees the original recipe card lying face-down on the kitchen table. Mistaking it for scrap paper, he jots down the grocery list on the back and later trashes it. Grandma realizes what has happened and frantically calls her five friends to get the recipe, but amazingly, all five have also lost their copies!

Fortunately, her friends remember to call their daughters who are able to provide nine of the ten original copies.

Grandma compares the nine copies and finds a few misspellings, transposed words, and grammatical errors. However, she is still able to accurately assemble the original recipe because even though minor errors crept in, the same errors don't occur on each copy (it is highly unlikely the daughters would make identical errors). By cross-checking the copies, she can confidently identify the errors and re-create an accurate copy.[6]

This shows how scholars test ancient Bible documents.* Even if some copies contain errors, become damaged, or are altered by a copyist, an accurate record can still be assembled by comparing the thousands of other manuscripts found all over the world. Even copies with errors would not all have the same errors (see illustration opposite page). Errors and corruption will stand out against the huge number of manuscripts that agree. (There are over twenty five thousand New Testament and roughly fourteen thousand Old Testament manuscripts and fragments.)[7] The vast majority of surviving Bible manuscripts have only minor variances between them (in most cases, merely single words) and *no variances that affect meaning.***

#2. Ordinary & Extraordinary

If the skeptic asks us what makes the Bible so special, we might pique his interest with this response:

"I believe the Bible came from God for two ORDINARY reasons and for two EXTRAORDINARY reasons."

If the Bible can be trusted for practical, ordinary information then it is *relevant*. If it can be trusted regarding supernatural, extraordinary information, then it is *authoritative*.

---

*This method is called textual criticism. Footnotes in most Bibles identify ambiguous words or phrases that appear in some manuscripts and not in others.
**Ehrman disagrees, but his inflated and sometimes manufactured arguments against selected passages dissolve in light of the passages he ignores.[8]

Variances in Copies of Grandma's Recipe

Blackberry Sauce

2 pt. fresh blackberries, halved
1/4 cup sugar
2½ tsp. orange zest
½ tsp. ground ginger
1 pt. vanilla ice cream
6 gingersnaps, crushed

1) Stir together first 4 ingredients in a sauce pan over med. high heat; cook, stirring constantly, 5 minutes or until thoroughly heated.
Serve over ice cream; sprinkle with gingersnaps

Even if there are variances between the recipe copies, we could still assemble an accurate recipe because the same mistakes do not appear on all copies, and there is a preponderance of information on which all copies agree.

Blackberry Sauce
Serves 6
2 pt. fresh blackberry, halved
1/4 c sugar
2½ tsp orange zest
½ tsp. ground giner
1 pt. vanilla icecream
6 gingersnaps crushed
Stir together first 4 ingredients in a sauce pan over med. heat, cook 5 min. stir constantly until heated.
Serve over icecream w/ gingersnaps.

Blackberry Sauce
2 pt. fresh blackberries, halved
1/4 cup sugar
2½ tsp orange zest
½ tsp ground ginger
1 pt. vanilla icecream
6 gingersnaps, crushed

Stir together first 4 ingredients in a saucepan over medium heat, cook, stirring constantly, 5 minutes or until thoroughly heated. Serve over vanilla icecream; sprinkle with gingersnaps.

Blackberry Sauce
2 pt. fresh blackberries, halved
1/4 cup sugar
2½ tsp. orange zest
½ tsp. ground ginger
1 pt. vanilla ice cream
6 gingersnaps, crushed

1. Stir together first 4 ingredients in a saucepan over medium heat; cook stirring constantly, 5 minutes or until thoroughly heated. Serve over vanilla ice cream; sprinkle with gingersnaps

Variances such as:

"med. high heat"
v. *"medium heat"*,

"stirring" v. *"stir"*,

"c" v. *"cup"*,

"sprinkled"
v. *"sprinkle"*,

and " " v. "1."

...do not corrupt the recipe.

Ordinary

1) The Bible is **honest about people.**
2) The Bible is **historically accurate.**

Extraordinary

1) The Bible **predicts specific future events.**
2) The Bible was written by forty authors over fifteen hundred years, **yet its teachings are seamlessly consistent.**

ORDINARY REASONS

1) The Bible is **honest about people**.

It accurately depicts human nature (sinful but redeemable) and records the feats and failures of its heroes (Abraham, Jacob, Jonah, David, Peter, etc.)

This is perhaps the most relatable aspect of the Bible. Even if they don't accept the extraordinary evidence, they might identify with the humanity of the Bible. This reason also answers the objection, *"The Bible writers were biased."* If they were biased, why would they include the most unflattering details about heroes of the Bible?

2) The Bible is **historically accurate**.

If it does not agree with recorded history, then we can't trust it.

Secular records and archaeology repeatedly verify the Bible's accounts of people such as King David, Pilate, the Hittites, many others and details of places such as Sodom, Gomorrah, Nineveh, Nazareth, and Rome.[9]

But there are many good books on human nature and history, so that alone isn't convincing. The Bible should give us something beyond that, otherwise, why should we trust it above other books? The next two reasons set it apart.

EXTRAORDINARY REASONS

1) The Bible **predicts specific future events.**

It includes something supernatural that is also verifiable by recorded history. Hundreds of years before the events, the Bible predicted:

- The Persian King Cyrus 100+ years before his birth (Isa. 44:28, 45:1)

- The rise of four specific world powers (Dan. 2:37-40; 8)

- Nebuchadnezzar's destruction of mainland Tyre and unique defeat of island Tyre by Alexander the Great's coalition over 250 years after Ezekiel's prophecy (Ezek. 26).[10]

- The four-way division of Alexander's kingdom (Dan. 11:3-4)

- Jesus' crucifixion (Ps. 22)

2) The Bible was written by forty authors over 1,500 years yet **its teachings are seamlessly consistent.***

- The consistent character of God across both Testaments:
  - God's compassion: Jon. 4:11, Ps. 78:37-38 vs. Mat. 9:36, 11:28-30
  - God's judgment: Deut. 30:15-18 vs. Mat. 7:21-23, John 2:15

- Consistent themes across both Testaments:
  - Blood atonement: Lev. 17:11 vs. Heb. 9:22
  - Unblemished lamb: Ex. 12, Isa. 53:7 vs. Luke 23:4, John 19:33
  - Only son of miracle birth as a sacrifice: Gen. 22:2 vs. John 3:16
  - Virgin birth: Isa. 7:14 vs. Mat. 1:25
  - Justification by faith (not works): Gen. 15:6, Hab. 2:4 vs. Gal. 2:16, Eph. 2:8
  - Self identification of God: Ex. 3:14 vs. John 8:58
  - Final judgment: Dan. 12:2 vs. Mat. 25:46

- The complementary (not contradictory) accounts of Jesus' life, death, and resurrection in the four Gospels.

*This reason takes longer to unpack than the others. If the skeptic offers any specific examples of biblical inconsistency, ask him if he would be willing to let you explain them from the Bible.

"Odd, the way the less the Bible is read the more it is translated."[1]

- C. S. Lewis

12: BIBLICAL RED-FLAG WORDS

People who seldom open the Bible have some of the strongest opinions about it. The skeptic's words in this chapter indicate a general mistrust of the authenticity of the Bible. These words express the generalizations of biblical skeptics who seldom have specific examples to support their claims.

Here are some key words to clarify objections concerning the Bible's reliability:

- "LEGEND"/"MYTH"
- "LITERALLY"
- "TRANSLATIONS" (of the Bible)

"LEGEND"/"MYTH"

SKEPTIC'S MEANING

Any event in the past that cannot be explained naturalistically

Legends don't just pop up overnight. They take several generations to develop and to overtake historical fact.[2] It is difficult to pass along a legend as fact when people who witnessed the events are alive to refute it. Jesus' resurrection is a prime example. Mark wrote his account of the empty tomb only thirty years after Jesus' crucifixion. The other three Gospels were completed within thirty years after Mark. Plenty of people were alive to dispute the empty tomb but none did (although the Pharisees contrived a story to explain it [Matt. 28:12-13]). More significantly, Paul repeats a creedal statement about the resurrection in 1 Corinthians 15:3-8 that even staunch Bible critics date to within *one to three years* after Jesus' resurrection–no time for a legend to have developed.*

---

*Even critics who question the credibility and authorship of the four Gospels, support Paul's authorship of 1Corinthians and seven other N.T. books. This makes the creed repeated in 1 Corinthians significant.[3]

"LITERALLY"

<u>SKEPTIC'S MEANING</u>

Having a simplistic, wooden understanding of the Bible

> "It's a waste of time to argue with fundamentalists.
> And this film doesn't do it. It's designed for
> intelligent people who are willing to change their mind.
> And of course, one film is not going to change
> religious life in America, but it will give intelligent people
> who want to read the Bible in a modern way a chance.
> If we insist on reading the Bible literally,
> in 25 years nobody will read it any longer."
>
> - William Dever, biblical consultant for the PBS film, *The Bible's Buried Secrets*[4]

The objection, *"You don't read the Bible literally, do you?"* is a smug retort that characterizes conservative Christians as naïve or uneducated. It suggests that evangelicals robotically absorb every biblical word in a one-dimensional, wooden fashion while "intelligent people" read it with sophistication. But a disdain for reading the Bible "literally" reveals a skeptic's presumptions about passages rather than his examination of them. In fact, the objection itself shows that the skeptic may not be as sophisticated as he presumes to be.

To read anything accurately, we must read it *literally* (i.e., according to the context, structure, purpose, and background in which it was written). Informed Christians recognize that the Bible is full of literary devices and figurative language such as metaphor, simile, metonymy, typology, allegory, personification, and so forth. The difference between us and most skeptics, including the Bible scholars popular media selectively consult, is that we don't dismiss out of hand the supernatural elements like they do. Just because the content of a passage seems unlikely to modern-day secularists (Jonah being swallowed, the Red Sea parting, etc.) doesn't make it figurative. Jumping to a naturalistic reading of a book

To read anything accurately, we must read it *literally* (i.e., according to the context, structure, purpose, and background in which it was written).

that claims to be divine (2 Tim. 3:16)* and that has the historical credentials to prove it, shows that literary considerations have taken a backseat to twenty-first-century presumptions.

"TRANSLATIONS" (of the Bible)

SKEPTIC'S MEANING

The many conflicting biblical texts we have now versus what was originally written down

When a skeptic refers to differences in Bible "translations," he may be questioning *transmission*. Most accepted Bible translations (New International Version, New American Standard, King James, etc.) differ in paraphrasing, not content. Translations rely on the accurate transmission of the Bible from the original languages into English or whatever the receptor language happens to be. However, transmission determines if the Bible we have today is the same one that was written in the original languages.

Discoveries such as the Dead Sea Scrolls are significant because the Scrolls are one thousand years older than manuscripts previously found of the same Old Testament books, yet they are virtually identical to them. This shows clean preservation of content over one thousand years, a powerful example of how carefully the Bible has been transmitted throughout the centuries.

*All Scripture is God-breathed and is useful for teaching, rebuking, correcting and training in righteousness. See also Gal. 1:11-12, 1 Thes. 2:13, and 2 Pet. 1:20-21.

BONUS POINTS

I. Why Does God Allow Suffering?

If the skeptic is in the midst of suffering, be careful about offering words of wisdom (see Job's friends); just listen. However, if he really wants to know why God allows suffering or is questioning God's character, ask the MORAL Probing Question, *"What is your standard for right and wrong?"* (i.e., what moral standard are you using to judge God?). Explain that because God gave us moral freedom, suffering and evil are real possibilities resulting from our choices (the biggest choice being that of Adam and Eve to disobey God, thus bringing pain and suffering into the world). If we were only able to choose good, then we wouldn't be free.

You might ask the skeptic how often we thank God for every moment of good compared to how often we complain to Him about the bad. As Job said, *"Shall we accept good from God, and not trouble?"* (Job 2:10).

You could also point out that we can't see the whole picture and that God may be using difficult situations to reveal Himself (as Jesus explained when the disciples asked why a man was born blind [John 9:3]). What may be a bad situation for one person could bring out the good in others. But accepting this requires trusting God which is difficult for a skeptic to do if he hasn't attempted to know Him.

II. Bible Fundamentals

The Bible declares that, *"All Scripture is God-breathed and is useful for teaching, rebuking, correcting and training in righteousness"* (2 Tim. 3:16), but some parts more easily equip us in the fundamentals than others. It is helpful to understand what the Bible says about these concepts: *the nature of God, the nature of man, sin, salvation,* and *creation.* Start with the following five areas of the Bible:

1) **Genesis** - the foundations of sin, redemption, marriage, etc.

2) **The Law** (Exodus-Deuteronomy) - how God is set apart
(holy) and how the many O.T. laws foreshadow the perfection
required to reach Him that only Christ ultimately fulfills

3) **The Gospels** - what Jesus said about Himself; His
crucifixion and resurrection

4) **Romans** - the extent of sin; salvation (a free gift); grace
versus works

5) **Paul's Letters** - Galatians (faith not works); Colossians
(Jesus is fully God)

III. Rhetoricals and Hypotheticals

Suppose you get a rhetorical objection like the one my
friend asked me about the virgin birth, "...*you don't really
believe that, do you?*" This kind of objection assumes there is
an obvious but unstated reason *not* to believe the question at
hand, but it removes the skeptic's responsibility to explain why
he doesn't believe it. So just ask him, "*Why don't you believe
_____?*" From there, keep asking questions until you
focus the conversation on the Root Idea.

Another common way objections are presented is in
the form of hypothetical situations such as, "*What about people
in remote places who have never heard of Jesus?*" Don't get
side-tracked by hypotheticals. The Bible gives a clear answer
to this question,* but it is not the immediate concern. The real
issue is not what the person in a remote place is going to do
with Jesus, God, or truth; it is *what is the skeptic to whom
you're speaking* going to do with them. Keep the focus of the
conversation on him.

IV. Jesus' Claims to Divinity

The following is a good sampling although not
necessarily a comprehensive list of Jesus' explicit or implicit
claims to be God. It is powerful to be able to refer to a few of
these in case you are challenged:

*God set the times and places in which everyone would live (Acts 17:26-27). Psalm 19:1-4
and Romans 1:19-20 state that every people group is aware of God's glory through
creation. Romans 2:14-15 describes God's law written on every heart. These internal
and external witnesses make everyone accountable to God.

Matthew: 5:17; 10:32-33; 11:27; 12:6-8; 13:41; 16:27; 19:28; 22:42-45; 23:34; 26:64; 27:43; 28:18
Mark: 2:5; 9:31; 14:61-62
Luke: 5:22-24; 7:48-50; 9:20-21; 10:22-23; 18:19; 21:27; 22:67-71; 24:7
John: 5:16-18,23; 8:23-25, 58; 10:30; 12:45, 20:26-29
...also **Revelation** 1:18.

V. Can't Christians Believe in God-guided (Theistic) Evolution?

Theistic evolution is perhaps the worst of all possible explanations. As discussed in Chapters 9 and 10, according to existing scientific principles, flawed evolutionary theory, and fossil evidence, *evolution does not work and has not happened.* In the Bible, either God allows nature to operate according to the *working* laws He already set in place (e.g., genetic limits–creatures produce after their *own kind*) or He overrides natural laws altogether (changing water to wine, raising the dead). *But He does not establish broken principles* such as evolution and make them work despite themselves.

More significantly, Christians who buy into evolution usually don't recognize its theological implications. Evolution means that death existed *before* sin, (millions of years of creatures died while the most adaptable ones evolved until man appeared). But the Bible declares that *man's sin preceded death* (Gen. 2:17; Rom. 5:12; 1 Cor. 15:21).[1]

In the evolution model, death is a natural part of existence. But death is *not* a natural part of God's created order; it is the ultimate penalty for man's sin and is an enemy of God Himself (*"The last enemy to be destroyed is death"* [1 Cor. 15:26]). Paul tells us in Romans that *"the creation itself will be liberated from its bondage to decay"* and that we *"groan inwardly as we wait eagerly for our adoption as sons, the redemption of our bodies"* (Rom. 8:21, 23).* Why would our bodies and creation at large need to be liberated or redeemed

---

*These verses and Rom. 8:22 make it clear that death afflicted the entire creation, not just man.

if death were part of God's original order? Jesus describes His own death as a *ransom* (Matt. 20:28), a price paid to free slaves or captives. If our death were part of God's original created order, there would be no debt in need of payment; our spiritual account with God would already be balanced.

VI. Evidence for Bible Reliability

The basic tests for the reliability of ancient documents are as follows[1]:

Manuscript evidence

The reliability of an ancient manuscript is determined by the number of manuscript copies that still exist, the amount of time between the copies and the original, and the consistency between these copies. We have no original ancient manuscripts by Homer, Julius Caesar, Thucydides, nor any of the Bible. Yet, compared to the many famous ancient works whose reliability is unquestioned, the Bible has by far the most manuscript evidence and the shortest time gap between the originals and the copies. This places its reliability in a class by itself.

Internal evidence

Are the events recorded truthfully? How close to the events historically and geographically was the author? Does the author contradict himself? Does the author appeal to hostile as well as to friendly witnesses to verify his account? An author such as Luke who explicitly states his intentions to record an "orderly account" (Luke 1:3) provides excellent testimony for the credibility of the written record.

External evidence

External evidence includes historical sources besides the Bible that substantiate its records. What archaeological discoveries confirm people and places described in the Bible? What events documented in secular history prove Bible prophecies? Many ancient historians such as Josephus, among others, provide corroboration for the events recorded in Scripture.

RESOURCES

Reading these Christian thinkers will enrich your understanding of what has been discussed in this book. In alphabetical order:

Jay Budziszewski	Phillip Johnson	Alex McFarland
G. K. Chesterton	Peter Kreeft	R. C. Sproul
William Dembski	C. S. Lewis	Lee Strobel
Norman Geisler	Irwin Lutzer	Frank Turek
Ken Ham	Josh McDowell	Ravi Zacharias

Here are reading suggestions for four great introductory resources corresponding to each worldview category:

SPIRITUAL: *A Ready Defense* - Josh McDowell [reference book; short sections on each world religion]

MORAL: *Relativism: Feet Firmly Planted in Mid-Air* - Francis J. Beckwith and Gregory Koukl [170 pgs.]

SCIENTIFIC: *Defeating Darwinism by Opening Minds* - Phillip Johnson [131 pgs.]

BIBLICAL: *More than a Carpenter* - Josh McDowell [128 pgs.]

QUICK REFERENCE CHART

SPIRITUAL SKEPTICISM

WORLDVIEW:
Spirituality

ROOT IDEA:
"Good works get you heaven."

PROBING QUESTION:
*"How good is good enough
(to get you to heaven)?"*

MORAL SKEPTICISM

WORLDVIEW:
Relativism

ROOT IDEA:
**"People should decide for
themselves what is right
or wrong."**

PROBING QUESTION:
*"What is your standard for
right and wrong?"*

QUICK REFERENCE CHART

SCIENTIFIC SKEPTICISM
WORLDVIEW:
Naturalism

ROOT IDEA:
"The natural world is all that there is." *(Nature can do godlike things.)*

PROBING QUESTION.
"How much faith is required for that belief?"

BIBLICAL SKEPTICISM
WORLDVIEW:
Secularism

ROOT IDEA:
"The Bible is man-made."
(It originated with man rather than God)

PROBING QUESTION:
"If God gave us a book, how would we know it really came from Him?"

END NOTES

Chapter 1: Making Your Faith Relevant

1. Collins, Brian. ed.*When in Doubt, Tell the Truth: And Other Quotations from Mark Twain*. Columbia University Press, 1997. 67 p. Google Book Search. 8 Jan. 2008 <http://books.google.com/books?id=5oWFmBHH00wC&pg=PA67&dq=%22second-hand+from+other+non-examiners+whose+opinions+about+them+were+not+worth+a+brass+farthing.%22&sig=CvEYR_u2S6eD5B2t3lHLoy4k4YA#PPP3,M1>

2. *Monty Python and the Holy Grail* (1975). Prod. Michael White. Dir. Terry Gilliam, Terry Jones, Perf. Graham Chapman, John Cleese, Terry Gilliam. DVD. Sony Pictures, 2001.

3. Zacharias, Ravi. "Reaching the Happy Thinking Pagan." *Just Thinking* Fall (1995) 8 Jan. 2008 <http://www.rzim.org/resources/jttran.php?seqid=30>

Chapter 3: Speak Their Language

1. Barker, Kenneth. gen. ed. *The NIV Study Bible - New International Version*. Grand Rapids: Zondervan Publishing House, 1985. text notes: Psalm 4:7, Matt. 5:8. 790, 1449 pp.

2. Dean, Curt. "Inerrancy of Scripture: Lesson 2." *Theology 101*. Course notes. 2 p.

3. Puig, Claudia. "Spiritual Carrey Still Mighty Funny." *USA Today Online*. 20 May 2003 <http://www.usatoday.com/life/2003-05-20-carrey_x.htm>

Chapter 5: The Spiritual Root Idea

1. Hubbard, L. Ron. "Doctrine of the Scientology Religion: Ch. 2." 4 Oct. 2007. <http://www.bonafidescientology.org/Chapter/02/page01.htm>

2. Black, Nathan. "Poll: 9 of 10 Americans Believe in God; Nearly Half Rejects Evolution." *The Christian Post*. 2 Apr. 2007. 8 Jan. 2008 <http://www.christianpost.com/article/20070402/26658_Poll:_9_of_10_Americans_Believe_in_God%3D_Nearly_Half_Rejects_Evolution.htm>

3. Zahid, Ishaq. *Islam 101*. "Five Pillars of Islam." Sunday, 10/5/2008= 4 Shawwal, 1429 AH. 19 Oct. 2007 <http://www.islam101.com/dawah/pillars.html>

4. "Watchtower Doctrine Exposed." Witnesses for Jesus. 14 Oct. 2007 <http://www.4witness.org/jehovahs_witness/jw_exp.php>

5. Zacharias, Ravi. *Jesus Among Other Gods*. Nashville:Word Publishing. 2000. 90 p.

6. Fay, William and Ralph Hodge. *Share Jesus Without Fear*. Lifeway Press, Nashville. 1997. 45 p.

Chapter 6: Spiritual Red-Flag Words

1. "The Gospel According to Oprah." *Watchman Fellowship*. excerpted from July 1998 *Vantage Point*. 2 Oct. 2007.
<http://www.wfial.org/index.cfm?fuseaction=artNewAge.article_1>

2. Barry A. Kosmin and Ariela Keysar (2009). "American Religious Identification Survey (ARIS) 2008" (PDF). Hartford: Trinity College. Accessed 2011-07-28. 2 p.

3. Barna Group, The. "Barna Survey Examines Changes in Worldview Among Christians over the Past 13 Years." *Barna Group*. 6 March 2009
<http://www.barna.org/barna-update/article/21-transformation/252-barna-survey-examines-changes-in-worldview-among-christians-over-the-past-13-years>

4. Hughes, Dennis. "An Interview with Mark Victor Hansen." *Share Guide*. 2004. 5 Jan. 2007 <http://www.shareguide.com/Hansen.html>

5. Ibid.

6 *Ron Howard: 50 Years in Film*. Turner Classic Movies television special. Dir. Schickel, Richard. 29 Dec. 2008

7. "Lexicon Results for *qadash* (Strong's H6942)." *Blue Letter Bible*. 30 Dec. 2007.
<http://cf.blueletterbible.org/lang/lexicon/lexicon.cfm?Strongs=H06942&Version=kjv>

8. "Lexicon Results for *hagios* (Strong's G40)." *Blue Letter Bible*, 30 Dec. 2007.
<http://cf.blueletterbible.org/lang/lexicon/lexicon.cfm?Strongs=G40&Version=kjv>

9. Lewis, C. S. *Mere Christianity*. New York: Macmillan Publishing Company. 1970. 39 p.

10. Our Eyes Are Open Ministries, "The Church of Oprah Exposed." YouTube video. 26 Mar. 2008. <http://youtube.com/watch?v=JW4LLwkgmqA>

Chapter 7: The Moral Root Idea

1. Lennon, John. "Give Peace a Chance." *The John Lennon Collection*. Prod. John Lennon, Yoko Ono, Phil Spector. EMI. 1982.

2. *Star Wars: Episode III, Revenge of the Sith*. Prod. Rick McCallum. Dir. George Lucas. Perf. Ewan McGregor, Natalie Portman, Hayden Christensen. DVD. Lucasfilm Ltd. 2005.

3. "MTP Transcript for Oct. 22: Barack Obama, David Broder, Charlie Cook, John Harwood, Robert Novak." *Meet the Press with Tim Russert*. 2006.
<http://www.msnbc.msn.com/id/15304689/page/2/>

4. Turek, Frank. "Deconstructing Liberal Tolerance: Relativism as Orthodoxy." Audio tape. Impact Apologetics. 2003.

5. Geisler, Norman. "What Is Truth? Is It Absolute?" Lecture. *Truth for a New Generation Conference*. 18 Mar. 2003.

Chapter 8: Moral Red-Flag Words

1. O'Donnell, Rosie. *The O'Reilly Factor*. Fox News Channel. 30 Mar. 2002.

2. Beckwith, Francis J., and Greg Koukl. *Relativism: Feet Firmly Planted in Mid-Air*. Grand Rapids: Baker Books. 1998. 2 p.

3. Geisler, Norman. "What Is Truth?"

4. "Self-Defeating Statements." *The Coffee Place's Joke Stack*. <http://www.thecoffeeplace.com/Jokes/aaaaabsi.html>

5. Geisler, Norman. "What Is Truth?"
(reference applies to this and previous five bullet points.)

6. Zacharias, Ravi. "The Spurious Glitter of Pantheism." *Let My People Think*. Radio broadcast. 14 May 2006. (attributed to a number of sources).

7. Bronner, Ethan. "After 50 Years of Covering War, Looking for Peace and Honoring Law." *The New York Times/ Week in Review*. 16 Dec. 2001. 29 Dec. 2005. <http://www.nytimes.com/2001/12/16/weekinreview/16WORD.html?ex=1136005 200&en=f6b08b59a6eef71d&ei=5070>

8. Copan, Paul. *True for You but Not for Me*. Minneapolis: Bethany House Publishers. 1998. 35 p.

9. John Paul II, Pope. "Homily in Orioles Park at Camden Yards." 8 October 1995 <http://www.catholic-forum.com/saints/pope0264is.htm>

10. Chesterton, G. K. as quoted in *Autobiography*. Collected Works Vol. 16, p. 212. *The American Chesterton Society*. 5 Jan. 2007. <http://www.chesterton.org/qmeister2/17.htm>

11. Zacharias, Ravi. "Absolute Truth in Relative Terms." *Let My People Think*. Radio broadcast. 2 Dec. 2007.

12. Walker, Peter J. and Tyler Clark. "Tony Jones. *Relevant Magazine*. Issue 32. March-April 2008. 69 p.

13. Beckwith. 147 p.

14. Beckwith. 68 p.

Chapter 9: The Scientific Root Idea

1. Dembski, William. *The Design Inference*. Cambridge University Press, 1998. 55 p. Google Book Search. 27 Aug. 2008 <http://books.google.com/books?id=R7otNWMrgcwC&pg=PA55&dq=%22Yet+h ere+we+are–as+a+result,+I+believe,+of+spontaneous+generation."&sig=ACfU 3U1HO6zJlyShp8skwJgQWQcKsR5CjA#PPA55,M1>

2. Lowenstein, J., and Adrienne Zihlman, Ph.D. "The Invisible Ape." *New Scientist.* 120(1641) 1988:56, 57. <http://animatematters.blogspot.com/2006_05_01_archive.html>

3. Geisler, Norman. "Miracles and Modern Scientific Thought." Truth Journal. 14 July 2002.
<http://www.leaderu.com/truth/1truth19.html>

4. Lisle, Jason, Ph.D. "God & Natural Law." AnswersInGenesis.org. August 28, 2006. Accessed 27 Aug. 2008
<http://www.answersingenesis.org/articles/am/v1/n2/god-natural-law>

5. Batten, Don. "Where Are All The People?" AnswersInGenesis.org. Accessed 6 Jan. 2008. First published: *Creation* 23(3):52–55June 2001
<http://www.answersingenesis.org/creation/v23/i3/people.asp>

6. McLeod, Dan. *The Georgia Straight.* "Interview with Jodie Foster." 10-17 July 1997:43 (as reported by Celebrity Atheist List).
<http://www.celebatheists.com/index.php?title=Jodie_Foster>

7. Dembski, William A. *Intelligent Design.* Downers Grove: InterVarsity Press. 1999. 91, 106 p.

8. Catalano, John. "The 'Know-Nothings,' The 'Know-Alls,' and the 'No-Contests': A Lecture by Richard Dawkins extracted from *The Nullifidian."* Dec. 1994
<http://www.simonyi.ox.ac.uk/dawkins/WorldOfDawkins-archive/Dawkins/Work/Articles/1994-12religion.shtml>

9. *The Planet of the Apes.* Prod. Mort Abraham. Dir. Franklin J. Schaffner. Perf. Charlton Heston, Roddy McDowall, Kim Hunter. 20th Century Fox. 1968.

Chapter 10: Scientific Red-Flag Words

1. Batten, Don. "Gould Grumbles About Creationist 'Hijacking."
AnswersInGenesis.org. Aug. 2002. 8 Jan. 2008
<http://www.answersingenesis.org/tj/v16/i2/idea.asp>

2. Gitt, Werner. "What about the Big Bang?" AnswersInGenesis.org. Creation Archive: Volume 20 Issue 3. 3 Jan. 2008
<http://www.answersingenesis.org/creation/v20/i3/big_bang.asp>

3. Sarfati, Jonathan. "Who's Really Pushing 'Bad Science'?" AnswersInGenesis.org. 26 Sept.2000. 21 Oct. 2007
<http://www.answersingenesis.org/news/lerner_resp.asp>

4. Dembski, William A. *Intelligent Design.* Downers Grove: InterVarsity Press. 1999. 128-146, 159-174 p.

5. Dembski, 10 p.

6. Dawkins, Richard. *The Blind Watchmaker*. Norton, 1996. 21 p. (online book). 22 Oct. 2007
<http://macroevolution.narod.ru/dawkins_watchmaker/watchmaker.html>

7. Behe, Michael J. *Darwin's Black Box: The Biochemical Challenge to Evolution*. New York: Free Press. 2006. 42-43 pp.

8. Dembski, William A. "Still Spinning Just Fine: A Response to Ken Miller." v.1. 17 Feb. 2003.
<http://www.designinference.com/documents/2003.02.Miller_Response.htm>

9. Dembski. "Still Spinning Just Fine."

10. Johnson, Phillip. *Defeating Darwinism By Opening Minds*. Downers Grove: InterVarsity Press. 1997. 72-73 p.

11. Konotey-Ahulu M.D., Dr. Felix. "Sickle-cell Anaemia Does Not Prove Evolution!" Creation Archive: Volume 16 Issue 2. 28 Oct. 2007.
<http://www.answersingenesis.org/creation/v16/i2/anaemia.asp>
and
Leslie Ph.D., J. G. "In Brief–D.N.A. Mutation and Design." Creation Archive: Volume 6 Issue 4. 3 Jan. 2007
<http://www.answersingenesis.org/creation/v6/i4/mutation.asp>

12. Wells, Jonathan. *Icons of Evolution*. Dir. Brian Boorujy. Perf. Steve Meyer, Paul Nelson, Jonathan Wells. DVD. Randolph Productions Inc., 2002.

13. Dawkins, 21 p. *The Blind Watchmaker*.

14. Ibid. 317 p.

15. Wieland, Carl. "Muddy Waters: Clarifying the Confusion about Natural Selection." AnswersInGenesis.org. June 2001. 21 Oct. 2007
<http://www.answersingenesis.org/creation/v23/i3/muddywaters.asp>

Chapter 11: The Biblical Root Idea

1. Sproul, R. C. *Renewing Your Mind with R. C. Sproul*. "Here and Now." Podcast. 7 Dec. 2009

2. Tucker, Neely. "The Book of Bart." WashingtonPost.com. 5 March 2006. D01 p.
<http://www.washingtonpost.com/wp-dyn/content/article/2006/03/04/AR2006030401369.html>

3. Ibid.

4. "Americans: My Faith Isn't the Only Way to Heaven." Accessed 24 June 2008
<http://www.foxnews.com/story/0,2933,370588,00.html>

5. Kreeft, Peter and Ronald Tacelli. *Handbook of Christian Apologetics*. Downers Grove: InterVarsity Press. 1994. 151 p.

6. Koukl, Greg. "Can We Know for Certain That the New Testament Has Been Handed Down Accurately?" *Solid Ground*. Jan./Feb. 2005. 2 p.

7. Hanegraaff, Hank. "The Reliability of the Bible/Perspective: CP1000." CRI. 3 Jan. 2007
<http://www.equip.org/site/c.muI1LaMNJrE/b.2548569/k.C763/The_Reliability_of_the_Bible.htm>
and
Hanegraaff, Hank. "M-A-P-S to Guide You through Biblical Reliability: Statement DB011." CRI. 16 Nov. 2007
<http://www.equip.org/site/c.muI1LaMNJrE/b.2635115/k.AED8/DB011.htm>

8. Wallace, Daniel B. "A Summary Critique: Is What We Have Now What They Wrote Then? A Book Review of *Misquoting Jesus: The Story Behind Who Changed the Bible and Why* by Bart D. Ehrman." Review: JAB111.
<http://www.equip.org/site/apps/nlnet/content3.aspx?c=muI1LaMNJrE&b=4127933&content_id=%7BA5EDD865-C37A-4CD8-9310-1765F1F3D23A%7D&notoc=1>

9. McDowell, Josh. *A Ready Defense*. Nashville: Thomas Nelson Publishers. 1993. 92-117 pp.

10. Kennedy, D. James. *Why I Believe*. Nashville: Word Publishing. 1999. 4-7 pp.

Chapter 12: Biblical Red-Flag Words

1. Lewis, C. S. "Quotes by C.S. Lewis." *The C.S. Lewis Society of California*. as quoted in Letters of C. S. Lewis from 25 May 1962. <http://www.lewissociety.org/quotes.php>

2. Hanegraaff, Hank. *Resurrection*. Nashville: Word Publishing. 39 p.

3. Habermas, Gary. "The Evidence That Changed a Generation." Lecture. *The National Conference on Christian Apologetics 2007*. 7 Nov. 2007.

4. West, Jim. "Billy the Dever, PBS, And 'The Bible's Buried Secrets'." *Dr. Jim West: Bible and Theology*. 22 July 2008.
<http://jwest.wordpress.com/2008/07/22/billy-the-dever-pbs-and-the-bibles-buried-secrets/>

Bonus Points (V): Can't Christians Believe in God-Guided (Theistic) Evolution?

1. Ham, Ken, and Andrew Snelling. *The Answers Book*. Green Forest, AR: Master Books. 1998. 90 p.

Bonus Points (VI): Evidence For Bible Reliability

1. McDowell, Josh. *More Than A Carpenter*. Wheaton: Living Books. 1977. 47-57 p.

Meet the Skeptic can be easily taught to church groups, families, and ministry partners. Lead your team with these additional resources:

Workbook
$4.99 | 978-0-89051-659-1

Leader Guide
$7.99 | 978-0-89051-667-6

MEET THE
AUTHOR

As a Christian apologist and owner of a brand image and design firm, **Bill Foster** has a unique perspective of how the popular culture perceives and is influenced by the ideas that shape our world. He has created an approach for engaging skeptics that breaks down objections into categories. Bill believes that understanding the worldviews behind these categories, rather than chasing down answers to every objection, is the key to reaching the heart of a skeptic's thinking.

MEETTHESKEPTIC.COM
FACEBOOK.COM/**MEETTHESKEPTIC**
TWITTER.COM/**MEETTHESKEPTIC**

HigherWerks
brand image | design

higherwerks.com